GOD HATES SUFFERING

GOD HATES SUFFERING

His Compassion is Our Commission

Dr. Bryan R. Davenport

VANCOUVER, WASHINGTON
MARCH 2016

Copyright © 2013 by Dr. Bryan R. Davenport
All rights reserved
ISBN: 1530953650
ISBN 13: 9781530953653

CONTENTS

Introduction	God Hates Suffering	vii
Chapter 1	My Personal Story	1
Chapter 2	The Problem	4
Part One	Compassion, Commission and Confidence	7
Chapter 3	The Compassionate Kingdom	9
Chapter 4	Does God Will Sickness for Our Own Good?	17
Chapter 5	The Importance of Compassion	21
Chapter 6	His Compassion is Our Commission	26
Chapter 7	The Compassionate Conduct of the Commissioned	32
Chapter 8	What Happens If We Experience Defeat?	39
Chapter 9	Our Confidence for the Commission	42
Part Two	Common Sense Compassion: Everyday Approaches to Helping the Hurting	49
Chapter 10	Command, Contact and Climate	51
Chapter 11	Approaching Healing	57
Chapter 12	Approaching Deliverance	63
Chapter 13	General Principles for Deliverance	70
Chapter 14	Conclusion	73
Chapter 15	God Hates Suffering	74
	Sources Consulted	77

INTRODUCTION

GOD HATES SUFFERING

Hate is a strong word. Charged with emotion, it is a feeling of intense hostility toward a thing. Society tells us we aren't supposed to hate – that hating things is evil. On the contrary, it seems appropriate that some things should be hated. Some things deserve to be hated. Furthermore, you can tell a lot about someone by what they hate. God hates suffering.

When I say "hate" I do not mean that which comes from fear. God is afraid of nothing. When I say "hate" I refer to that which rises from the furnace of God's burning affection and unfailing love. When I say that God hates suffering, I refer to the deep, visceral, divine response and resolve to defend and deliver the object of God's eternal affection.

When I say "suffering," I do not mean challenge, discipline or hard work. These things, the normative struggles of life, though often unpleasant, are not suffering. They are growing pains, challenges to overcome, the stewardship of responsibility. We dig. We plant. We push. We clock-in. We sweat. We pay taxes. We mow the lawn. We write term-papers. We have dead-lines. We work. Work is a gift from God. I don't believe that even the Garden of Eden was a "sweat-less" place. God has no dislike for labor or sweat or even frustration. All of these things (again, unpleasant at the time) prove vital to the enlargement of our joy and the achievement of purpose in life.

So, when I say suffering, I mean that which results from sin, sickness, sadness, poverty, oppression, and torment. I mean injustice. I mean everything for which Christ died. And in this book, when I say suffering I mean sickness, disease and the tyranny of the devil. I mean the evil of suffering. God hates suffering.

When I say that God hates suffering, I mean that He opposes it, fiercely, out of compassion. In every act of God's saving intervention, He has exercised compassion. Jesus, the centerpiece revelation of the nature of God, never prescribed suffering as a means toward piety or peace. He never answered suffering with an admonition to cope, but with an act of compassion.

Every movement of God's Spirit through the ages since the birth of the church at Pentecost has included divine demonstration of compassion. Every Spiritual awakening through the centuries has inspired men and women to confront the sickness, oppression and injustice of their era.

When I say that God hates suffering, I say it with the certainty provided by the Son of God, by the Spirit of God and the Scriptures.

How you believe God feels, and how strongly and specifically you believe that He feels about suffering will influence how you feel. What you believe that He's done about suffering will influence what you do about it. It will influence how you feel about sickness or oppression in your life, in your home and family. And it will influence how you view and what you do about sickness and affliction in your community – and on the earth.

In the pages that follow, I hope to demonstrate how God feels and what He has done about sickness and oppression. Further, I intend to show what God expects us to do, and how He has enabled us to do it. We will start with asking how we can know best what God is like, and how we can know with clarity His feelings toward suffering. The answer revolves entirely around the person and work of Jesus Christ: His compassion and commission.

Jesus Christ compassionately confronted sickness and torment with power. Further, He not only addressed symptoms of suffering, but He dealt with suffering at its core and cause. He cancelled the power of sin, defeated death, hell and the grave, and reconciled us to God. And then He charged His church to continue His work in the same way, by the same Means.

The goal of this book is to heat your heart with the same compassion of heaven, and then compel you to partner with heaven to confront and combat suffering on every level.

If you are a Christian, then you host the hope of the whole earth. Draw a line. You will either explain, accommodate and cope with suffering, or you will pray, contend and make war against it with compassion and power. What you believe about how God feels will influence how you feel. And what you believe God has done will influence what you do.

Let me start with sharing how this book came to be.

1

My Personal Story

It was a Sunday evening service. My family was sitting in the very last pew in the back of the auditorium. I do not recall why we were sitting there, because the Davenports were not back-seat-sitters. But God may have providentially assigned our seats on this occasion. It was a "Sunday Night Healing Service" in the Assembly of God church we had just returned to after helping to plant a different church across town. I was quite young. I do not recall my exact age, but I could not have been more than eight years old.

Sitting in the back, I could see the pageant play out in front of me. A man was shouting "JESUS!" into the ear of someone who apparently could not hear, or at least could not hear a few moments ago. I sensed something in the room—something that was different. There was a presence that felt heavy and warm. My mother must have explained to me that it was a healing service and that the man in the front was a guest minister, because I would not have extrapolated those facts on my own.

It was the next scene that unfolded before my young eyes that burned my conscience indelibly. A distinguished gentleman walked down the center aisle of the church, carrying the limp body of a bone-thin, unconscious female. I could see tears streaming down his cheeks. Again, my mother must have explained what was happening. She was the man's daughter, and she could not walk or talk. That daddy was carrying his daughter up to the altar for prayer—so that the man yelling "JESUS!" at the front could try to help her.

I do not remember what happened next. If the girl recovered, I am certain I would have remembered it. However, I do remember what I felt deeply in those immediate moments. A blend of emotions and convictions settled profoundly upon my young psyche. My first emotion was a sense of great hope—Jesus was a healer. Although healing was not something I could fully grasp, I knew it was beautiful and powerful. I knew that people needed healing, and I knew Jesus was the way. Ironically, I also felt a strong sense of injustice. In my young mind, it was not right that the near-lifeless lady remained that way. It was not right that her daddy had those tears. It was not right. I felt the painful paradox of hope and injustice.

From that moment, healing and the ministry of healing permeated my thoughts and affections. Stories in the gospel of Jesus' healing the hurting burned like coals in my soul. Even animated portrayals of Jesus' ministry brought me to tears. There was something very special about healing.

As years progressed, I grew up hearing stories of miracles but saw very few of them. My church did not seem to believe or embrace the miraculous very strongly. Healing was clearly affirmed by doctrine, but much less-so by demonstration. Somewhere along the way, the concept that healing was difficult settled into the landscape of my consciousness. This feeling did not come from my devotional reading of Scripture. Instead, disappointment and fear formulated their own theology. So I lived most of my life believing in and hoping for healing but remaining deeply afraid of failure and void of confidence in my own "use-ability" by the Lord.

Then, when I was an adult with a family of my own, the doctor called. My oldest child, my son, was diagnosed with an incurable, degenerative condition that could take his life (if unhindered). Our world crashed. I searched Scriptures for how I should respond. I honestly was not certain what I should feel or what posture I should take. Perhaps God was allowing this for our good? Was I to accept that this illness was from His hand? I turned to the Gospel stories. I genuinely had no agenda but to listen for something—for anything the Lord would have me be or do or feel. I looked up each passage in the Gospels in which a parent had a sick or suffering child. I would seek my counsel there. I found a consistent response. Jesus never left a child suffering. He never declined a parent's petition for help. Even in the face of apparent failure, or death, Jesus tells a panicked parent, "Do not be afraid; only believe" (Mark 5:36).[1]

A resolve arose in my heart. I knew there were things I did not know or understand. But I did know God's nature revealed in Christ. I knew the truths Jesus revealed. God hates suffering; Jesus is a healer.

I also recognized that there are a host of differing approaches and methods regarding healing. I observed that the more people attempted to learn new keys, steps, or formulas, the more frustrating the ministry of healing became for believers. However, compassion is not complex. If believers could understand healing and its concurrent partner, deliverance, shaken loose from the baggage of well-intended clumsy theology, then God could help more people, and more people could help others.

---

1   All Scripture quotations, unless otherwise noted, are from the New International Version.

2

THE PROBLEM

Jesus models healing and deliverance as a principal expression of His Kingdom. In His commission, He mandates this ministry to His followers. The message of forgiveness and reconciliation to God through Christ must include a concurrent confrontation of suffering. Without a doubt, healing and deliverance communicate and confirm the message and mission of Christ. But they also flow from the heart and nature of God. They are not merely polemics, convincing the beholder of divine reality. They are normal expressions of a loving, compassionate Savior-Redeemer. Despite the biblical models and mandates, both churched and un-churched people remain in need of healing and deliverance.

Those who engage in these ministries of healing and deliverance often seem inexplicably to conduct themselves in eccentric ways, inviting distance and suspicion. Even if practitioners avoid eccentricity, mainstream ministry leadership easily marginalizes them, if only because what they practice falls outside the routine of evangelicalism. Finally, many schools of thought reject any notion of contemporary healing or deliverance, relegating all such works to first-century Christendom.

Traditional Pentecostal or Charismatic attitudes and approaches to healing and deliverance are also problematic, both in terms of expression and experience (giving and receiving). Most approaches over-emphasize style, culture, or formula, leaving a residue of frustration. Many believers may desire to engage in these ministries, but they often lack the comfort or confidence and feel under-equipped to approach those in need of healing and deliverance. As a result, believers often neglect or forfeit these principal kingdom ministries and perceive them as the property or practice of a select few, so these ministries of compassion remain elusive and exclusive.

Leaders need to encourage believers so that they feel more comfortable and confident in sharing the loving power of Christ to those in need of healing and deliverance. This will require a modification of traditional attitudes and approaches to healing and deliverance. Believers need to understand healing and deliverance as expressions of divine love. Further, it is necessary to replace the litany of complex formulas and methods with common-sense, biblical-based approaches. With a fresh perspective of this ministry, and the comfort and confidence necessary, believers may indeed give and receive it "freely."

This book seeks to promote confidence and participation in all forms of compassionate ministry, but two main applications serve as foci: healing and deliverance. For the purpose of this book, I will use these terms to indicate the following:

Healing: (1) The cure, removal or significant reduction of disease, sickness, and physical or emotional pain; and (2) The partial, ongoing, or full restoration of physiological processes damaged or lost due to disease, sickness or incident.

Deliverance: (1) The divine removal of oppressive, harassing spiritual influences; and (2) The act of helping another person experience freedom from spiritual bondage.

I will proceed with a positive assumption with regard to the need and validity of healing and deliverance in contemporary settings. I will address some concerns and confront some common objections without presenting either a full polemic or apologetic for these ministries. The focus of the book is less "argument for" and more "encouragement of." As the thrust of this project seeks to frame healing and deliverance as normal expressions of the nature of God and loving actions congruent with His nature, I will take all pains to avoid the introspection and fault-finding often accompanying discussions of healing. Further, I will not engage in forensic debate over labels or doctrinal distinctions. The subject will remain centered upon receiving and expressing the compassion of the Kingdom.

This book should prove helpful on several levels. It should help the Church to shift the focus of ministering healing and deliverance from formula, style, and specialization to everyday expressions of joyful love. Further, more believers should feel greater degrees of comfort and confidence in ministering healing and deliverance. They will root their confidence in sound biblical principles and values. Ultimately, this book should result in believers helping more of those who are suffering find hope and help in the Name of Jesus. Using key biblical passages, I will seek to provide a biblical-theological basis for this confidence by demonstrating the source and supply of this assurance in (1) the nature and mission of the kingdom of God, (2) the commission of the Church, and (3) the anointing of the Holy Spirit.

Part One

Compassion, Commission and Confidence

3

THE COMPASSIONATE KINGDOM

WHAT IS THE KINGDOM OF GOD?

OUR UNDERSTANDING OF and approach toward suffering begins with what we believe to be true about the Kingdom of God. What is His Kingdom? What does it do? How do we know?

To begin with, God's Kingdom is His dominion, His saving rule. It is less a location in time or place as much as it is His influence over both. M. J. Harris explains that the Kingdom of God is "His eternal saving sovereignty ... His kingdom is His saving action; the realm where His salvific rule is exercised."[1] R. T. France writes, "The 'kingdom' is dynamic, not static. It is not a 'thing' that exists; it is God ruling, exercising rule."[2] Pause for a moment and reflect on the gravity of what these scholars assert. If the Kingdom of God is the realm where His salvific rule is exercised; if it is God exercising His rule, then how should we respond to the idea that Jesus enjoined us to pray that His Kingdom would come...on earth as it is in heaven? (Matt. 6:10).

---

[1] M. J. Harris, "Salvation," in *The New Dictionary of Biblical Theology* (Downers Grove, IL: Intervarsity, 2000), 763.

[2] R. T. France, "The Gospel of Matthew," *The New International Commentary on the New Testament* (Grand Rapids, MI: Eerdmans, 2007), 148.

In the Gospels, Jesus announces God's rule, calling for repentance and faith: The time had come; the Kingdom had arrived; all who heard should repent and believe the good news (Mark 1:15). The preaching of the Kingdom heralds the promise of forgiveness of sins (Luke 24:47), and it includes restoration of relationship with God and believers' adoption as His children (Gal. 4:4-7). According to William Hendrickson, the gospel of the Kingdom "indicates God's kingship, rule or sovereignty, recognized in the hearts and operative in the lives of His people, effecting their complete salvation ... i.e. all the spiritual and material blessings—blessing for the soul and body—which result when God is king in our hearts, recognized and obeyed as such."[3]

So the message is that the Kingdom of God has come and brings a totality of transformation into our lives. God has brought His rule upon us. But how might we understand the nature of the Kingdom more specifically? How might we have confidence to know what affect the Kingdom "intends" toward us – especially with regard to sickness, disease and demonic oppression?

To understand the Kingdom, we need only to look to the King.

---

3   William Hendricksen, "The Gospel of Matthew," *New Testament Commentary* (Edinburgh: Banner of Truth, 1973), 249.

THE KING REVEALS THE KINGDOM

As King, Jesus *perfectly* and *powerfully* demonstrates the nature and mission of the kingdom of God. Jesus claims that His words and actions are the direct expression of the will of God (John 5:19; 10:30, 32, 37-38; 14:7, 10-11)[4]. These passages affirm with clarity and certainty that what Jesus said and did were the perfect expression of the will and work of His Father. Rodney A. Whitacre points out that Jesus' words in John 5:19 (whatever the Father does, likewise the Son does) reveal "the Semitic version of the ideal son, since a son is to reproduce his father's thought and action," explaining that Jesus means "his source of being and activity is not himself but his father."[5] Whitacre suggests that Jesus' claim in John 10:30 of oneness with the Father is speaking of "God's love, care and power and his own claim to share in these."[6]

Paul declares that Jesus is the image, or icon, of the invisible God (Col. 1:15), and is "in very nature God" (Phil. 2:6). The writer of Hebrews claims that though God spoke in various ways in the past, that "God has spoken

---

4   John 5:19, "Jesus gave them this answer: "Very truly I tell you, the Son can do nothing by himself; he can do only what he sees his Father doing, because whatever the Father does the Son also does.

John 10:30, "I and the Father are one."

John 10:32, "but Jesus said to them, "I have shown you many good works from the Father. For which of these do you stone me?" (In John's Gospel, the word "works" refers to the miraculous works of Jesus.)

John 10:37-38, "Do not believe me unless I do the works of my Father. [38] But if I do them, even though you do not believe me, believe the works, that you may know and understand that the Father is in me, and I in the Father." (Note that Jesus points to the works that He does in order to understand the Father).

John 14:7, 10-11, "If you really know me, you will know[a] my Father as well. From now on, you do know him and have seen him....Don't you believe that I am in the Father, and that the Father is in me? The words I say to you I do not speak on my own authority. Rather, it is the Father, living in me, who is doing his work. [11] Believe me when I say that I am in the Father and the Father is in me; or at least believe on the evidence of the works themselves." (Note again how Jesus implores His audience to consider His works in order to see the Father.)

5   Rodney A Whitacre, "John," *The IVP New Testament Commentary Series* (Downers Grove, IL: InterVarsity Press, 1999), 126.

6   Ibid., 270

to us by His Son" and that "the Son is the radiance of God's glory and the exact representation of His being" (Heb. 1:2-3). Ray C. Stedman comments, "God's word through the Son is final and complete."[7] Therefore, the person and work of Jesus must principally influence an individual's understanding of the Kingdom. People can see and learn from Jesus all they need to observe and know about His Kingdom. Thus, Kingdom theology must adhere to and be congruent with the life, words, and work of Jesus. Jesus is the template, the model, the picture of the Kingdom of God.

In a profound manner, Jesus demonstrates the mission of the Kingdom through His powerful, compassionate confrontation of suffering, specifically with regard to illness and oppression. Luke records Peter's summary of the ministry of Jesus with these words, "God anointed Jesus of Nazareth with the Holy Spirit and power, and he went about doing good and healing all who were under the power of the devil, for God was with him" (Acts 10:38).

In the Kingdom, healing and deliverance are expressions and consequences of the compassion of God. The ministry of Jesus demonstrates this compassionate confrontation of suffering. There is no clearer, more compelling evidence that God hates suffering than the works of Jesus.

A COMPASSIONATE KING: HEALER AND EXORCIST

Matthew introduces the ministry of Jesus to his readers when he says that Jesus went throughout Galilee teaching in the synagogues and preaching the good news of the Kingdom. Concurrent to the *proclamation* and *explanation*, He demonstrates a powerfully compassionate *confrontation* of illness and oppression. Jesus' mission is a comprehensive assault against suffering (Matt. 4:23-24). Jesus' compassion affects every area of peoples' lives. Joel Green notes that this compassion is complete, stating, "At the same time Matthew records people being restored to health, he records people being restored to

---

[7] Ray C. Stedman, "Hebrews," *The IVP New Testament Commentary Series* (Downers Grove, IL: InterVarsity Press, 1992), 21.

status within families and communities, the reordering of life based on faith in God, and the driving back of demonic power."[8]

Matthew first states that Jesus heals every sickness and disease, and then he delineates the forms of suffering Jesus relieves, including disease, pain, paralysis, and epilepsy. Squarely in the middle of the list of ailments, Matthew includes those oppressed by demons. This should not be understood as a restricted or specific list, but rather illustrates that Jesus' ministry was not limited to one or two ailments, and that Jesus was able to overcome even the most formidable malady. Craig Keener adds, "Jesus not only explained and proclaimed the Kingdom; he demonstrated God's authority by healing the sick and expelling demons."[9] Jesus' confrontation of suffering includes fighting all manners of illness and oppression. David Turner writes, "Matthew views the healings and exorcisms performed by Jesus as evidence for the presence of God's reign."[10] John Wimber agrees:

> Jesus validated His ministry from the perspective of a power demonstration of the Kingdom of God ... A close look at Scripture reveals that Jesus spent more time healing and casting out demons than preaching . ... Except for discussion about miracles in general, the amount of attention devoted to the healing ministry of Jesus is far greater than that devoted to any other aspect of His ministry.[11]

The compassionate works of Jesus dominate the record of His ministry. C. H. Dodd writes, "If we open the Gospels at almost any place, we cannot avoid encountering the miracles of Jesus."[12] Graham Twelftree explains that the re-

---

8   Joel B. Green, *The New Dictionary of Biblical Theology* (Downers Grove, IL: InterVarsity, 2000), 537.
9   Craig S. Keener, *A Commentary on the Gospel of Matthew* (Grand Rapids, MI: Eerdmans, 1999), 155.
10 David L Turner, "Matthew," *Baker Exegetical Commentary on the New Testament* (Grand Rapids, MI: Baker, 2008), 235.
11 John Wimber, *Power Evangelism*, rev. ed. (London: Hodder & Stoughton, 1992), 93.
12 C. H. Dodd, "Miracles in the Gospels," *Expository Times* 44 (1932-33): 507.

cord of Christ's miraculous activity serves to amplify the presentation of Jesus' character when he states, "In ancient biographical writing there was a deeply-rooted convention that what a person did was an important part of summing up the character of that person."[13]

Jesus even violates religious taboos in order to confront others' suffering, including physically touching a leper (Mark 1:41) and a dead girl (Mark 5:41). Grant Osborne calls Jesus' willingness to break religious taboos and traditional demands whenever He sees a need as the "hermeneutic of love."[14]

Matthew repeatedly testifies to Jesus ministering healing to crowds of people. In Matthew 12:15, "A large crowd followed him, and he healed all who were ill." In 14:34-36, he crosses over to Gennesaret, and when "the men of that place recognized Jesus, they sent word to all the surrounding country. People brought all their sick to him and begged him to let the sick just touch the edge of his cloak, and all who touched it were healed. Great crowds come to Jesus in 15:30, and "bringing the lame, the blind, the crippled, the mute and many others, and laid them at his feet; and he healed them." And again in 19:2, Jesus heals the "large crowds" who followed him. Considering the volume of Jesus' compassionate ministry Matthew includes throughout his text, it is clear that the confrontation of suffering is central to the mission of the Kingdom of God.

While healing often takes precedence in discussions of the ministry of Jesus, His deliverance of those under the torment of demons also expresses His compassion. Exorcism is just as central in Christ's mission as healing. Keener reasons: "While it is almost an indisputable fact that Jesus preached and healed, the volume of evidence makes it extremely likely that Jesus actually had a reputation as an exorcist."[15] Did you catch that? Consider the significance of this assertion against the mild-mannered Jesus too often portrayed in paperback books. The first miracle Mark records is Jesus driving out

---

13 Graham Twelftree, *Jesus the Miracle Worker: A Historical and Theological Study* (Downers Grove, IL: InterVarsity, 1999), 19.

14 Grant R. Osborne, "Matthew," *Zondervan Exegetical Commentary on the New Testament* (Grand Rapids, MI: Zondervan, 2010), 157.

15 Keener, *Commentary on the Gospel of Matthew*, 155.

an unclean spirit from a man in the synagogue (1:21-26). And then, because of this specific work, "His fame spread everywhere..." - because of an exorcism.

Keener goes on to explain, "The record does not always make the boundary between healing and exorcism clear. ... The language of healing could include exorcism in the ancient Jewish circles."[16] Therefore, particularly in the instances in which "mass" healings occur, one may accept the likelihood of deliverance from demons occurring as well. Factoring in the language Peter uses in Acts 10:38,[17] one should allow for biblical authors to describe Jesus' confrontation of the concurrent conditions of illness and oppression with one word—"heal."

So significant is the expulsion of demons to His ministry that Jesus identifies it as a keynote of the Kingdom. In Matthew 12:28, Jesus claims, "If I cast out demons by the Spirit of God, then the Kingdom of God has come upon you."[18] In Luke 4:18, when Jesus announces that the Spirit of the Lord is upon Him, He uses language that positions Him as a liberator between the oppressed and their oppression, or oppressor. Charles Talbert says that when Jesus stands and quotes from Isaiah 61, He identifies Himself as an exorcist.[19] Twelftree asserts, "Not only does the conducting of miracles appear to dominate the activity of the historical Jesus; the exorcisms in particular loom large as one of the most obvious and important aspects of his ministry."[20] When Herod summoned Jesus, Jesus sent word that He was busy: "He replied, "Go tell that fox, 'I will keep on driving out demons and healing people today and tomorrow, and on the third day I will reach my goal'" (Luke 13:32).

According to Matthew 8:16-17, Jesus' ministry of healing and deliverance fulfills the prophetic depiction of the suffering servant's atoning work from

---

16 Ibid.
17 Acts 10:38 "Jesus went about doing good and healing all who were under the tyranny of the devil."
18 All Scripture references, unless otherwise noted, come from the New International Version.
19 Charles T. Talbert, *Reading Luke: A Literary and Theological Commentary on the Third Gospel* (New York: Crossroad, 1992), 56.
20 Graham Twelftree, *In the Name of Jesus: Exorcism Among the Early Christians* (Grand Rapids, MI: Baker Academic, 2007), 46.

Isaiah 53:4. As the crowd brings the ill and oppressed to Jesus, He drives out demons and heals the sick. Matthew recognizes and records the prophetic fulfillment. Hendricksen writes, "In this work of casting out demons and healing the sick, Matthew, by divine inspiration, sees a fulfillment of Isaiah."[21]

Lawrence Burkholder explains the relationship between Christ's atonement and His powerful confrontation of suffering:

> Evil in the fallen creation, including demonic infestation in persons, can only be cleansed through the death and resurrection of Jesus Christ. First, Jesus; life, death and resurrection and glorification broke Satan's claim on humanity. Second, Jesus' atonement has cut every curse which operates against humanity, including those which evil spirits use to gain access to persons. Third, Jesus' atonement confers and confirms God's immense love for humanity. The God who loved us enough … loves us enough to deliver us.[22]

Healing and deliverance are consequences of God's rule, secured by Christ's finished work on the cross, which powerfully and compassionately confronts suffering.

---

21 Hendricksen, 400.
22 Lawrence Burkholder, "The Theological Foundations of Deliverance Healing," *Conrad Grebel Review* 19, no. 1 (Winter 2001): 58.

4

DOES GOD WILL SICKNESS FOR OUR OWN GOOD?

EXCURSES ON SUFFERING AS FORMATION

DIFFERENT THEOLOGIES OF suffering, or paschologies, exist to varying degrees. One of the schools of thought is that God prescribes suffering for redemptive purposes, even for the formation or maturation of believers. It is not uncommon for believers to presume that sicknesses or infirmities are part of God's will for their betterment. While no specific passage of Scripture endorses illness as a divinely preferred tool for maturation, believers in particular might experience heightened spiritual awareness or stricter spiritual disciplines as a result of their illnesses. Further, they may find fresh perspectives on priorities or new value in relationships. It is not uncommon to hear heart-warming (or heart-wrenching) stories of how God "used" a painful period to produce something good. There is no denying that God may work any situation to His children's edification and advantage, regardless of the harshness or sadness of their circumstances. This is reason for thanksgiving: God is good in the midst of what is not good.

The problem, however, occurs when believers displace confidence for healing or recovery with the stoic resignation to accept their circumstances as the will of God. God's inherent, active goodness in the presence of affliction or suffering does not indicate His authorship or preference for these conditions. There is no evidence in the gospel narratives that Jesus prescribes illness or oppression for anyone's formation or maturation. Jesus never refuses compassion for anyone who suffers and comes to Him for aid.[1] On the contrary, the volume of testimonies from the life of Jesus shows He is compassionate and powerfully confrontational of human suffering.

An example used to depict physical suffering as God's will is Paul's description of his thorn in 2 Corinthians 12:7-10. Paul cites his "thorn in the flesh," which he has pleaded with God to remove, but He has not. Several common theories exist to explain this thorn as one form of illness or another. Philip E. Hughes notes that it is not possible to settle on an answer to the question regarding the identity of Paul's thorn: "It is another one of those questions which, on the evidence available, must remain unanswered."[2] James Garlow argues that the term, "thorn in the flesh" is Paul's use of a Hebrew idiomatic expression.[3] Garlow explains that, to Paul, a Hebrew, a thorn in the flesh carries a relatively certain meaning. In Numbers 33:55, Joshua 23:13 and Judges 2:3, some form of the expression "thorn in the flesh" refers to people who cause trouble—typically people opposed to the will of God with corrupt or malicious motives toward the people to whom they are "thorns."[4] In the context of 2 Corinthians 11:23-28, Paul seems to refer to people and the hurtful and harmful treatment he receives. Nowhere does Paul imply that God desires or delights in the treatment Paul endures. Rather, Paul argues that God's grace is more than sufficient to overcome. The last, very last thing we should interpret Paul's thorn in the flesh to be is an illness that God refused to relieve.

---

1 Jesus even rewards the Syrophoenician woman in Mark 7:25, whom He initially seemed to ignore, for her faith in His compassion, regardless of religious and racial taboos.
2 Philip E. Hughes, "The Second Epistle to the Corinthians," *The New International Commentary on the New Testament* (Grand Rapids, MI: Eerdmans, 1962), 442.
3 James Garlow, *God Still Heals: Answers to Your Questions about Divine Healing* (Indianapolis, IN: Wesleyan Publishing House, 2005), 106.
4 Ibid.

First Peter 4:1 advises believers to arm themselves with the same attitude as Christ, who suffered in His physical body, and prepare themselves to suffer likewise in their bodies. It would be, I argue, a grave error to assume that Peter is prescribing that his audience readily accept disease and demonic torment as part of their duty as followers of Christ. How could the Peter who beheld the miracles of Jesus, heard the repeated imperatives of Jesus to proclaim the Kingdom and perform cures (and raise the dead and drive out demons), and then who personally exercised the authority of Christ's name time again during Jesus' life time and then more so after Pentecost (Acts 3, Acts 5, Acts 9) – how could this Peter then turn around and endorse this sort of suffering? It defies logic.

Peter more likely refers to the kind of preparation in which believers prepare to endure suffering as persecuted people. I. Howard Marshall offers clarity on Peter's imperative, saying Christians should follow Christ's example. He argues, "A person who suffers shows that he has given up those things against which his suffering is a protest. In other words, by suffering Christ showed his opposition to sinful living. Therefore, persecuted Christians must follow his example."[5] Peter does not prescribe suffering. He spent his life confronting it.

Though the Church should prepare for persecution, it need not tacitly acquiesce to it. For example, Herod jails both Peter and James in Acts 12:1-5. Herod martyrs James, but the church prays Peter out of prison. James' tragic end did not convince the church to surrender, or to accept the same fate for Peter. The church, faced with the sorrow and loss of James, fights Peter's imprisonment with hope and resolute prayer. This is a sound example of biblical suffering and how to prepare for and contend against it. This story encourages contemporary believers who, though they may experience pain or the loss of a loved one, may still hope for and pray for victory for someone else who is suffering—even if from the same condition. If one church member loses his or her battle against cancer, for example, believers may—and should—face the next person's diagnosis with resolute hope. Losing James does not mean

---

5   I. Howard Marshal, "1 Peter," *The IVP New Testament Commentary Series* (Downers Grove, IL: InterVarsity Press, 1991), 133.

we must surrender Peter. We may not win every battle, but we should never retreat from the war.

James writes that believers should consider it joy when they face diverse trials (James 1:1). It is unlikely that James has illness in mind here, in light of how he addresses the issue of sickness specifically in the latter portion of his letter. In 5:16, James encourages those facing trouble to pray, presumably prayers that are confident of resolution (1:6). Those who are sick (5:14) should call for the elders to pray over them. By anointing them with oil and sharing prayers of faith (v. 15), the sick will be made well—God will raise them up. The Scripture passages leave open the possibility that the sick people may have sinned (v. 15b-16). Their sicknesses may be a result of sin. George M. Stulac offers that "the connection between sin and illness is a possibility, not a necessity in every case. ... The cure promised in 5:16 seems to encompass both physical and spiritual healing."[6] The text demonstrates that God no more desires the cause than He does the consequence. He forgives and heals. That is the nature of His Kingdom. Compassion confronts everything contrary to the will of God.

---

6   George M Stulac, "James," *The IVP New Testament Commentary Series* (Downers Grove, IL: InterVarsity Press, 1993), 182.

5

THE IMPORTANCE OF COMPASSION

Compassion is paramount in the practice of ministry. Jesus demonstrates not only God's great power but also His love. Few doubt that "if there is a god," he would indeed be strong. That is not a great revelation. The real revelation Christ brings is that this mighty God is also full of compassion, and compassion elicits faith. Apart from faith, it is impossible to please God (Heb. 11:6), but it is God's compassion that invites humankind to trust in Him.

The role of faith in receiving from God is important. James 1:5-7 encourages the believer to pray with confidence that it is God's nature to give but admonishes the petitioner to believe and not doubt. James warns that a double-minded man should not expect to receive from the Lord. But a problem arises when ministers present faith as a "work" or something for believers to "work up." To present faith as something God measures quantitatively in exchange for something good from the Lord is false and poisonous. Stulac warns that the result of this kind of teaching "is a crippling of people's faith and a perversion of the very truth James is teaching: that God gives freely, without finding fault."[1]

Jesus presents faith as something that displaces every other means of access. With Jesus, faith is "only" and "all" people need to receive. When Jesus

---

1   Stulac, 42.

says to the blind men in Matthew 9:27, "According to your faith let it be done to you," He does not add a condition, but He displaces all the conditions from the Mosaic Law required for healing. Instead of "if you will do," Jesus says, "because you believe." Craig Blomberg and Twelftree both argue that believers should understand "according to your faith" as "in response to your faith," not "in proportion to."[2] Jesus decrees that as these men believed, so God would grant it to them. Leon Morris understands this to mean that believers' faith is causative (because they believe) instead of congruent (in the measure they believe).[3]

Further, Jesus takes these two blind men aside, away from public view, to minister to them. After restoring their sight, He insists they tell no one. Because Jesus ministers to them in private, and then enjoins them to secrecy, it is unlikely that Jesus had any greater motivation than compassion. Jesus does not see these blind men as a means to an end.[4] He isn't proving His deity or drawing a crowd. He is confronting suffering. Ben Witherington notes, "Jesus wanted his cures to be acts of compassion, not spectacles meant to wow people into God's Dominion."[5]

It is common for ministers to emphasize the *metaphorical* meaning of miracles. People often frame and discuss the miracles of Jesus, in particular,

---

2 Craig Blomberg, "Matthew," *The New American Commentary* (Nashville, TN: Broadman, 1992), 163. See also Twelftree, *Jesus the Miracle Worker*, 120.

3 Leon Morris, "Mathew", *The Pillar New Testament Commentary* (Grand Rapids, MI: Eerdmans, 1992), 196.

4 This story is an example of Jesus ministering, apparently, solely for the benefit of the person in need. It is not the only example of this type of ministry, but it serves here as a point of observation. Often miracles are described in forensic terms—as proofs, supplying evidence for a larger argument. Miracles certainly do support the claims of the Kingdom, as they supported the claim of the King (John 14:11). But it is important not to limit their meaning to evidence proving a larger point. If only for this reason, that this line of reasoning may discourage the hurting person from hope for help unless God has some point to prove to someone. It would be more helpful to people if they understood healing primarily from a compassionate template and then appreciated for its evidentiary value.

5 Ben Witherington, III, "Matthew," *Smyth and Helwys Bible Commentary* (Macon, GA: Smyth and Helwys Publishing, 2006), 179.

as if they are parabolic—their primary purpose is not the act itself but the meaning behind the act.[6] Miracles do have messages. They have prophetic and eschatological implications. Old Testament prophetic literature often uses physical infirmity to illustrate destitute spiritual conditions (Isa. 29:9, 42:18). In one instance, Jesus claims that a miracle demonstrates His authority on earth to forgive sin (Matt. 9:6). However, even though physical conditions and the reversal of those conditions may communicate a larger meaning, the metaphor must not become the message. The spiritual application should not eclipse the compassion of the moment. It is difficult to imagine the lame (Matt. 9, Acts 3) or the blind (Matt. 20) immediately feel the spiritual or prophetic implications of their restored sight or new strength. It is far more likely that they are overwhelmed, and overjoyed, by the compassion of the King.

Regarding the importance of emphasizing compassion and its impact on believers' faith, F. F. Bosworth wisely teaches, "It is not what God can do, but what he yearns to do, that inspires faith. By showing his compassion everywhere in the healing of the sick, Jesus unveiled the compassionate heart of God to the people."[7]

Consider the example of the leper in Mark 1:40-45. When he approaches Jesus, the leper doesn't question Jesus' ability, but his willingness. "If you are willing, you can make me whole." As Jesus touches the man, he speaks to the leper's question: "I am willing; be made whole." Reading this passage away from the original language leaves the reader at, I believe, a disadvantage. This is because there are (at least) two common words for "will" (or "willing") in the biblical Greek. One of them, *baulomai*[8], denotes a passive acquiescence. It is a "willing" that expresses *permission*. Were this the word used in Mark 1, the result would have still been a man healed from leprosy. It would have been a record of Jesus giving permission, granting the request of the leper for healing without signaling any strong feeling in the matter. But there is another word

---

6   G. H. Twelftree, "Miracles in Mark," *The New Dictionary of Biblical Theology* (Downers Grove: InterVarsity, 2000), 777.

7   F. F. Bosworth, *Christ the Healer* (Grand Rapids, MI: Chosen Books, 1924), 74.

8   Strong's number 1014

for "willing," *thelo*[9], which means to be resolved, determined. It is an intimation of a Hebraism that means "to take delight, to take pleasure." When Jesus said to the leper, "I am willing" he was not expressing *permission*, but *preference*. In effect, Jesus answered with "I'd be delighted to make you whole. I prefer it." What kind of faith does this kind of compassion invite?

Matthew emphasizes the compassion of Jesus as he summarizes the ministry of Jesus in 9:35-36 using the same language he uses in 4:23, that Jesus was "healing every disease and sickness." In the Greek text, this phrase appears significant as it mirrors the LXX translation of God's covenant promises of healing and protection from disease in Deuteronomy 7:15. The Greek text of both Matthew 4:23 and 9:35 include the phrase, "*pasan noson kai pasan malkian.*" These are the same words in Deuteronomy 7:15, except the words for "sickness" and "affliction" are reversed. Craig Evans agrees with the intended connection between Matthew 4:23 and the LXX of Deuteronomy 7:15.[10] Also noting the similarity between Matthew's passage and the LXX is Barclay Newman and Philip Stone.[11]

It is not, I believe, any coincidence that Matthew appears to suggest that Jesus is the perfect reflection of Yahweh the Healer.

Matthew pauses to emphasize that Jesus sees the crowds and that he has compassion on them because they are "harassed and helpless, like sheep without a shepherd" (Matt. 9:36). Morris explains that this metaphor, "sheep without a shepherd," points to a people who are in great danger and without the resources to escape from it.[12]

Hendricksen notes that Jesus "restored them because he sympathized with them and loved them."[13] The original word that describes Jesus' response to the crowd is *splanchnizomai*, meaning a warm, compassionate response to

---

9   Strong's number 2309
10 Craig Evans, *Matthew*, New Cambridge Bible Commentary (New York: Cambridge University Press, 2012), 95.
11 Barclay M. Newman and Philip C. Stine, *A Handbook on the Gospel of Matthew* (New York: United Bible Societies, 1988), 99.
12 Morris, 239.
13 Hendricksen, 253.

need. There is no English term for this word. When Matthew uses this word, he relates not only an emotional response but also an action that meets a need. France writes, "It [compassion] is a word that describes the Jesus of the gospel stories in a nutshell."[14]

Jesus' compassion leads Him to further action, moving beyond ministering to the suffering by himself. Certainly, for every person Jesus touches, there are many more beyond His reach. He turns to His disciples and exhorts them to pray to the Lord of the Harvest to send out more workers (Matt. 9:37-38). Though the chapter ends here, the story continues.

Immediately, Jesus calls His disciples together for the express purpose of sending them out to do the very works of compassion He did during His time on earth (Matt. 10:1). Witherington summarizes Jesus' ministry, saying it is a prelude to the coming commission of Jesus' followers "to go and do likewise, imitating the words and actions of Jesus, thereby being extensions of Jesus' own ministry, Jesus' agents."[15]

---

14 France, 373.
15 Witherington, 207.

6

His Compassion is Our Commission

The previous section affirms the nature and mission of the kingdom of God, including the powerful, compassionate confrontation of suffering demonstrated in and by the ministry of Jesus. This section affirms the belief that Christ's compassion is the commission of the Church. The following section relates Jesus' instruction and impartation to His followers and the ongoing behaviors of those who carried His compassionate commission. Let's allow each Evangelist speak for themselves (all four Gospels include a compassionate commission).

Instruction and Impartation from Jesus

Matthew

In Matthew 9:35-36, the harassed and helpless[1] crowds move Jesus to compassion. His solution for their suffering is to gather His disciples and make His compassion their commission. Jesus calls the disciples to Himself and gives them the authority to drive out demons and heal every disease and sickness (Matt. 10:1). It is not coincidental that Matthew uses the same language

---

1   This phrase means that the crowds were oppressed under a force that they were unable to resist or escape from without external aid.

here to describe the commission of the disciples as he uses to summarize the ministry of Jesus in Matthew 4:23 and 9:35. Matthew makes it clear that the Kingdom is not limited to Christ's activity, but it is entrusted to His followers.

Fredrick Bruner explains, "Matthew wants us to see that Jesus' healing ministry ... has become the disciples healing ministry ... the disciples are to become the body of Christ—the extension of the incarnation. They are to carry out in their mission what Jesus carried out in his: exorcism, healing and later ... teaching."[2]

Jesus asks His followers to continue the ministry of the Kingdom. Witherington says that Jesus sends His followers out into the world like the *shaliach*—agents in early Judaism who represented the ones who sent them. The people of the time would say, "A man's agent is as himself."[3] Jesus sends His disciples out to do His works. He gives them power to drive out unclean spirits, heal the sick, cleanse lepers, and raise the dead. *Jesus makes no distinction between His work and the work He expects His followers to do.* Witherington confirms, "Jesus expects the twelve to do pretty much everything He was doing—teaching, preaching, [and] healing. The job description is not different. And furthermore, we may presume he made sure they were equipped to do what he asked them to do, not merely informed about what they ought to do."[4]

Matthew 10:7-8 picks up the instruction of Jesus. The passage offers concurrent charges to herald the arrival of the Kingdom—"the Kingdom of Heaven has come near"—and to compassionately confront suffering—"heal the sick, raise the dead, cleanse those who have leprosy, drive out demons." Jesus commissions the Church not only to preach and teach but to confront suffering in the same way He did. In fact, in this passage of Scripture (10:1-8), most of the instruction concerns the confrontation of suffering.

---

2   Frederick Dale Bruner, *The Christ Book: Matthew 1–12*, vol. 1 of *Matthew* (Grand Rapids, MI: Eerdmans, 2004), 452.
3   Witherington, 207.
4   Ibid., 228.

Other portions of Matthew also affirm that believers must pray for, proclaim, and practice on the earth the mission of God's Kingdom for the purpose of forming the former after the latter (Matt. 6:10, 10:7, 16:19, 18:18).[5]

Matthew's Gospel concludes with a reprise of Christ's commission to His followers (Matt. 28:18-20). This commission is similar to the previous commission, but there are at least two differences. First, in Matthew chapter 10, Jesus gives His disciples authority for ministry. But the authority becomes something altogether greater, because now Jesus has "all authority in Heaven and on earth." Second, instead of a localized mission to the people of Israel, the apostles must make disciples of every nation. Jesus does not *reduce* their commission in any way. Rather, He *expands* it *exponentially*, even to the end of the age.

LUKE

In Luke's version of the events in Matthew 10, Jesus gives His apostles the same instructions and impartation, except Luke uses the words "power and authority" in his passage (Luke 9:1). Jesus sends the apostles to drive out *all* demons and cure diseases. Luke's version of the commission is consistent with Matthew's charge to confront oppression and illness. Luke includes the concurrent activities of heralding the good news and compassionately confronting suffering (v. 6). Darrel L. Bock states, "The disciples' ministry mirrors Jesus' own ministry in Luke 8. Just as he preached the Word of the kingdom and healed, they are given authority over demons and disease as they seek to declare the kingdom of God."[6]

Luke's narrative departs from Matthew's when Luke includes a second mission trip (Luke 10:1). While Luke 9 includes only the initial twelve

---

5   This is a Kingdom-mandate principle in the book of Matthew. In this gospel, perhaps more clearly and emphatically than others, the reader sees that Jesus empowers and expects His followers to work to bring Heaven's realities to prevail upon the circumstances of earth. This is no more necessary than in the face of sickness, infirmity and demonic torment. These may not abide under Heaven's dominion.

6   Darrel L. Bock, "Luke," *The IVP New Testament Commentary Series* (Downers Grove, IL: InterVarsity Press, 1994), 162.

disciples, Luke 10 involves seventy-two[7] disciples. Jesus gives them the same command to announce the Kingdom and heal the sick (v. 9). There is no specific charge for disciples to cast out demons. However, when the missionaries return to Jesus, they do so with joy, exclaiming, "Lord, even the demons submit to us in your name" (v. 17). Although Jesus immediately directs their rejoicing to the paramount point that their names are written in the Lamb's book of life, it remains interesting that the sent-ones return from a mission of preaching and healing with reports of victory over demons. Walter L. Liefeld affirms, "The power of the kingdom was effective against demons just as it was in the ministry of Christ."[8] For the recipients, the commission to heal and announce the nearness of the Kingdom implicitly carries an expectation to confront and expel demons, or perhaps the confrontation of illness arouses reposing demons behind the afflictions. Either way, the missionaries drive out demons as part of their commission from Christ.

Contemporary churches should observe that deliverance is as much a part of the commission from Christ as preaching and healing. Obviously, exorcism stirs greater concern and hesitation, but the charge remains. Burkholder captures this sentiment when he writes, "It may make us flinch, but Jesus clearly put deliverance healing on His followers' agenda as a central sign of the Kingdom's reality."[9] Derek Prince insists that Jesus commits the same ministry to His followers; he argues that Jesus "never sent anyone out to preach the Gospel without specifically instructing and equipping that person to take action against demons in the same way that He Himself did."[10]

MARK

Similar to Matthew and Luke, Mark's Gospel provides a commission from Jesus to His apostles, which includes the heralding of the gospel message and

---

7 Or seventy, depending on the text source.

8 Walter L. Liefeld, "Luke," *The Expositor's Bible Commentary* (Grand Rapids, MI: Zondervan, 1984), 939.

9 Burkholder, 43.

10 Derek Prince, *They Shall Expel Demons: What You Need to Know about Demons–Your Invisible Enemies* (Grand Rapids, MI: Chosen Books, 1998), 10.

also presenting powerful works, including driving out demons and healing the sick (Mark 16:15-18). Believers commonly refer to this portion of Mark as the "longer" version, and serious doubt exists as to whether it was part of the original text. Many say someone added it later. If this is so, it was not significantly later, because the text has obvious ancient roots. Furthermore, if someone added the material, the content of the addition is consistent with the rest of Scripture. Among the potentially added material, there is an emphasis on the proclamation of the gospel and the powerful, compassionate confrontation of suffering. In response to the question of the authenticity of this portion of Mark, J. Lyle Story notes, "Christian writers of the second century such as Justin Martyr, Irenaues, and Tatian testify to the inclusion of these verses, and the earliest translations, such as the Latin, Syriac, and Coptic, all include them."[11] The most ancient users of Mark's Gospel include this "controversial" section that affirms the compassionate, powerful nature of the gospel.

JOHN

John's Gospel also includes a commission, but it only *implies* what the Synoptics *specify*. First, in the upper room discourse, Jesus promises His disciples that those who believe in Him will do what He has done and even "greater works" (John 14:12). Here Jesus makes a clear claim that He anticipates that His followers (without restriction—all who believe) will continue His works, even exceeding them. Whitacre recognizes Jesus' inclusive intent. He states, "Those who will do greater things are not just disciples to whom Jesus is speaking, but anyone who has faith in [Christ]." Whitacre offers that Jesus is saying, "Each believer will do what I have been doing."[12] As Osborne summarizes, "The church is to re-live the life and ministry of Jesus."[13]

After His resurrection, Jesus appears to His apostles and says to them, "As the Father has sent me, I am sending you" (John 20:21). Whitacre notes that "over forty times throughout the Gospel, Jesus is said to have been sent by

---

11 J. Lyle Story, "Mark" in *The New Spirit-Filled Life Bible*, ed. Jack W. Hayford (Nashville, TN: Thomas Nelson Publishers, 2002), 1380.
12 Whitacre, 354.
13 Osborne, 155.

God, and now that will become the characteristic of his disciples also."[14] The Greek language indicates that Jesus means "in the same way or manner I was sent, I am sending you." Jesus' mission includes a powerful, compassionate confrontation of suffering, and He sends His followers to do the same.

---

14 Whitacre, 479

7

THE COMPASSIONATE CONDUCT OF THE COMMISSIONED

THE GOSPEL NARRATIVES include and emphasize the expectation of Jesus that His followers will continue His works. Did they understand this? Did they "own" His compassion as their own? We need only observe the accounts and testimonies of the apostles and epistles to know this is true.

PETER AND THE FIRST GENERATION

The book of Acts narrates the story of how those Jesus commissions carry out their calling. In addition to proclaiming the message of the Kingdom to increasingly wider geographic and ethnic arenas, the apostles, and eventually others, continue Christ's compassionate ministry to the suffering. In the first example Luke provides in the book of Acts, Peter and John are on their way to the temple for a time of prayer (Acts 3:1-8) when a lame man petitions them for alms. Peter responds with a command and a helping hand, saying, "In the Name of Jesus Christ of Nazareth, walk." Fully healed, the man's response is overwhelming, joyful praise to God. When a crowd gathers in stunned amazement, Peter speaks to them about the healing and why it happened (v. 12).

Luke's language suggests that Peter may not have had a public message in mind until he notices the crowd's attention. Of course Peter is passionate about the proclamation of the gospel, but it seems quite possible that Peter's first instinct is to compassionately confront the suffering of the lame man. Only after he notices the crowd's response does Peter immediately, powerfully proclaim that in this act God has "glorified His servant Jesus" (Acts 3:13). This action glorifies Jesus' name because Peter shares a powerful act of compassion with one who is suffering. From this platform, Peter proceeds with a speech that becomes a template for apostolic preaching in Acts—Jesus anointed, crucified, raised, and Lord.

When Peter offers his defense before the Sanhedrin, he again refers to this as an act of compassion. He states, "If we are being called to account today for an act of kindness shown to a man who was lame and are being asked how he was healed, then know this ... it is by the Name of Jesus Christ of Nazareth" (Acts 4:9-10).[1] As the first specific example of personal ministry in the book of Acts, it bears the weight of influence, setting the tone and reference to understand the rest of the text. Clearly, the heralding of the gospel must include continuing compassion for the suffering.

As more and more men and women join the Church, the number of those who seek solutions to their suffering increases. As a result, Luke writes, "People brought the sick into the streets and laid them on beds so at least Peter's shadow might fall on them" (Acts 5:15). Crowds come even from the towns outside of Jerusalem, "bringing their sick and those tormented by impure spirits, and all of them were healed" (v. 16). Luke describes a compassion explosion. F. F. Bruce notes, "Even from outlying towns and villages of Judea people streamed into the capital with their sick folk in hope of profiting from the apostles' healing ministry."[2] Peter apparently does not preach or pray—just walks. Yet as one who carries the compassionate commission, he ministers healing and deliverance to everyone in his path. William J Larkin Jr. writes,

---

1   After this, Peter repeats the apostolic preaching template mentioned above.
2   F. F. Bruce, "The Book of Acts," *The New International Commentary on the New Testament* (Grand Rapids, MI: Eerdmans, 1988), 108.

"Whether during Jesus' ministry, or when the church is on mission ... God's power will effect a comprehensive healing when faced with human misery."[3]

Luke records more of this kind of ministry from Peter in Acts 9:32-42. While these stories provide inspiration for readers, they also confirm that leaders like Peter pick up where Jesus leaves off, ministering compassion to the suffering. There is no indication otherwise. Simon Kistemaker adds, "Jesus inaugurated the messianic age when he made the blind see, the lame walk, the lepers clean and deaf hear; when he raised the dead and preached the gospel to the poor. After Pentecost, this messianic age continues."[4] John Phillips adds,

> It was as if Jesus of Nazareth were back, as though He were there walking again—giving sight to the blind, making the deaf to hear, the dumb to talk, the dead to live, the lame to walk, cleansing the leper, casting out demons. And so He was. Only now it was His mystical body that was the vehicle of divine power rather than the material body in which He had lived when in the flesh.[5]

STEPHEN AND PHILLIP

As Luke continues the narrative, he delineates a democratization of the commission. Acts begins with a majority of the works of healing exercised by the original apostles, but along the way others pick up the same commission and confront suffering as part of their Kingdom expression. Stephen, a man appointed to help serve food to widows (Acts 6:1-4), performs great wonders and signs among the people (v. 8). Philip, one of the seven chosen with Stephen and part of those scattered after persecution breaks out, travels to Samaria to herald the news of the Kingdom (Acts 8:5). His proclamation of Christ, following the pattern Jesus provides, includes powerfully compassionate confrontation

---

[3] William J. Larkin, Jr., "Acts," *The IVP New Testament Commentary Series* (Downers Grove, IL: InterVarsity, 1995), 90.

[4] Simon Kistemaker, "Exposition of the Acts of the Apostles," *New Testament Commentary* (Grand Rapids, MI: Baker, 1990), 124.

[5] John Phillips, *Acts 1-12*, vol. 1 of *Exploring Acts* (Chicago: Moody, 1986), 62.

of the suffering in Samaria. Luke highlights, "For with shrieks, impure spirits came out of many, and many who were paralyzed or lame were healed. So there was great joy in that city" (vv. 7-8). The powerful works Philip performs draws the crowd's attention (v. 6), but the result is joy. Kingdom compassion produces joy.

NAMELESS MISSIONARIES

Others scattered by the same persecution travel further away. Luke pauses to mention Antioch, a location that will become a significant city-church in the unfolding narrative (Acts 11:19). Those who go to Antioch intentionally share the good news of Jesus with Greeks (Gentiles), which is a departure from the primarily Jewish mission. Luke tells his readers that "the Lord's hand was with them, and a great number of people believed and turned to the Lord" (v. 21). Luke's former reference to the "hand" of the Lord directly refers to healing and miraculous signs and wonders (Acts 4:30). It is entirely reasonable to conclude, given Luke's precedent in the text, that "the Lord's hand" includes works of deliverance and healing (Acts 5:12-16; 8:4-8). Among the many significant aspects of these events in Antioch, it is noteworthy that even those who Luke does not name perform powerful works. These are not celebrities, but they are servants.[6] Here is another example of the increasing democratization of compassionate ministry. Witherington writes that in the ministry of Jesus' followers, "Countless sick were healed, became recipients of God's grace, and heard the message of salvation."[7] F. F. Bruce confirms, "God was at work among them; they were witnessing the dawn of the new age."[8] It bears to reason that this trend should have continued, and contemporary believers should feel confident that Jesus also calls them to carry this same Kingdom-

---

6   I do not use the term "celebrity" with negative connotation but only to distinguish the historically famous names in Acts from these persons in Antioch whose names are not supplied.
7   Witherington, 686.
8   F. F. Bruce, "Acts," *New International Commentary on the New Testament* (Grand Rapids, MI: Eerdmans, 1988), 73.

commission of compassion as they confront suffering. Blomberg and Mariam Kamell agree: "The fact that miraculous healings continue after Jesus' resurrection, coupled with the lack of exegetical support for views that see gifts of healings as ceasing at the end of the apostolic age, suggests that believers in all eras may expect supernatural healings."[9]

Paul's Ministry

Paul, the self-confessed latecomer to apostolic ministry, ministers with no less power or compassion than his predecessors. Like his predecessors, his ministry includes deliverance and healing. In Philippi, Paul confronts the evil spirit tormenting and exploiting a young slave girl by commanding the spirit to come out of her in the Name of Jesus (Acts 16:17-18). While this act wins Paul no favor with those who profit from the slave-girl's oppression, it stands as an act of compassionate confrontation regardless of the consequences. Whether the audience responds with faith or resentment, Paul acts on behalf of the suffering for the sake of Christ.

In Ephesus, where Paul spends a considerable amount of time, God does extraordinary miracles. Luke explains that people take handkerchiefs or aprons from Paul's person and lay them upon the suffering, which cures their illnesses and makes the evil spirits leave them (Acts 19:11-12). While Luke does not appear to prescribe handkerchief ministry, the example reinforces the ongoing nature of powerful confrontation that accompanies Kingdom preaching and teaching.

Toward the conclusion of Paul's ministry as recorded by Luke, Paul experiences a horrendous storm at sea and shipwreck at Malta. Paul and his custodians become guests of the chief official of the island, Pablius. Paul visits Pablius' very ill father, lays hands on him and heals him. Afterward, Luke claims that the "rest of the sick on the island came and were cured" (Acts 28:7-9). Such a large expression of compassion is noteworthy and celebratory. In addition, it is curious that Luke does not mention preaching, invitations to

---

9   Craig Blomberg and Mariam J. Kamell, "James," *Exegetical Commentary on the New Testament* (Grand Rapids, MI: Zondervan, 2008), 171.

discipleship or conversions to faith among the Islanders. It is entirely reasonable to assume such activities take place given the precedent in the narrative of Paul's ministry. However, the fact that Luke takes time to include, and even emphasize, the healing of an entire island reminds believers that the Kingdom of God includes a powerfully compassionate confrontation of suffering. Last, this instance occurs in the latter portion of Paul's ministry. The power with which Paul ministers does not fade because it is a living and vibrant expression of the risen Lord and of His compassionate Kingdom.

PAUL'S CHURCHES

Most depictions of ministries to the suffering people in Acts occur in missionary contexts. Acts is a missiological narrative of the birth and expansion of the Church, so nearly all the events occur within that context. However, this does not mean that compassionate ministry occurs only on missionary frontlines. On the contrary, clues in epistolary literature suggest that while compassionate power signals the arrival of the Kingdom, it also remains the new normal for its citizens.

Paul reminds the Corinthian church that his first interaction with them includes preaching with the power of the Holy Spirit, so that their faith will rest on God's power (1 Cor. 2:4). Later, when Paul describes the church gathering for worship (presumably for their regular ongoing gatherings), he describes the Spirit ministering to and through the members of the community with various expressions of power, including faith, healing, and the working of miracles. These ministries are characteristic of the presence and power of the Spirit, who first greets believers and then remains in the church. God does not isolate these instances to missiological events (1 Cor. 12:1-11). Therefore, the inaugural events become normal. The same power initially present is theirs continually. Compassion is an ongoing part of the nature and function of the Church.

The book of Galatians provides an additional example. Paul also reminds the Galatian believers of the nature of his first ministry to them. He refers to their entrance into the Kingdom as "receiving the Spirit" (Gal. 3:3). It is logical to assume Paul's reference of the Spirit's presence here includes works of power. G. Walter Hansen agrees, "The reference to miracles in verse 5 is evidence that they also experienced outward manifestations of the Spirit's presence."[10] Gordon Fee offers, "[Paul] would simply not have understood the presence of the Spirit that did not also include such evidences of the Spirit's working that he termed 'powers' which we translate 'miracles.'"[11] After he reminds them of their initial experiences, Paul refers to their continuing experiences when he asks, "Does God give the Spirit and work miracles by the works of the law or by your believing what you heard?" (Gal. 3:5). Paul uses present tense verbs within this writing, indicating a present action. Again, those powers that ushered the believers into the kingdom remain part of their lives in that Kingdom.

The Church's commission to compassionately confront suffering as part of the Kingdom is missiological and ontological in nature. What it does for those new to or outside of the Kingdom it continues for those within the Kingdom.

---

10 G. Walter Hansen, "Galatians," *The IVP Testament Commentary Series* (Downers Grove, IL: InterVarsity Press, 1994), 79.

11 Gordon D. Fee, *Paul, the Spirit and the People of God* (Peabody, MA: Hendrickson, 1996), 166.

8

What Happens If We Experience Defeat?

Excurses on Frustrating Results

It is no secret that modern believers have claimed the principles Scripture prescribes and practice them on everyone from strangers to deeply beloved family members. But when contemporary believers do not see the results they anticipate or such hopes prove elusive, they may experience feelings ranging from frustration to heartache. In this circumstance, believers often choose one of two common alternatives. They may accept the condemning and condescending message that they lack enough merit or faith to secure the blessing they desire. The previous Scripture passages address this idea of lack of faith, and its inherent evil deserves no more attention in this text.

Believers may also choose to somewhat modify the apparent intent of Scripture texts to provide less literal meanings that more adequately conform to their experiences.[1] This is a dissonance-reducing measure that takes both God and the believer off the hook for the pain of disappointment. This approach may lead to a slippery slope of further reinterpretation of biblical texts to accommodate experiences—or even changes within popular culture.

---

1 Warren Weirsbe, "The Prayer of Faith," in *James*, vol. 2 of *The Bible Exposition Commentary* (Colorado Springs, CO: Cook Communications, 1989), 382-383.

However, compassion is not a performance, nor is it elective. The commission to compassionately confront suffering is a matter of obedience and love. Compassion is not conditional. One must not cease compassion in the face of delay, or even apparent failure. Compassion does not quit. Compassion keeps praying, believing, hoping, and caring for the suffering. Blomberg and Kamell offer this encouragement: "We ought to pray boldly, believing that He is a God of power and love and that He listens to the prayers of His people."[2] Compassion keeps the commission.

Paul's depiction of the nature of love in 1 Corinthians 13:7-8 sublimely supports this attitude by stating, "[Love] always protects, always trusts, always hopes, always perseveres. Love never fails." All the verbs in this passage are present tense active verbs, indicating action that is continuous. Compassion *always* protects, *always* trusts, *always* hopes, and *always* perseveres. Love bears up under people's sufferings to protect them. Love covers their pain and even covers the stigma or labels society may place upon them. Compassion confronts the suffering continually and comprehensively. Compassion does not quit.

Compassion treats every obstacle as temporary. Conditions do not summarize or identify people, but rather God's love for them forms and establishes their identities. Those who are suffering are ultimately image-bearers, and anything else is temporary. Their infirmity is not their identity or their destiny. Compassion treats people in view of their creation, their redemption and their eternity. No tumor, no disability, no pain should define one who is created in the image of God, redeemed by the blood of Jesus, and sealed for eternity by the Holy Spirit.

Love does not choose between natural and supernatural means of compassion. The Church should apply this "both/and" approach in as many ways as feasible. Those confined to wheelchairs should be able to have total access to houses of worship and prayer lines. They should have adequate seating and access to the facilities. Care should be taken to attend to the needs of the hearing or sight impaired. Functions and events should be organized in ways

---

2 Blomberg and Kamell, 244.

that take into consideration those with physical challenges. Believers should redeem every opportunity to do good. We ought not make it difficult for people to access hope, nor create structures that remind them of their challenges.

I have a son with a life-threatening disease that is deteriorating his body and makes it impossible for him to walk. So, each night I lay hands on my son, and I bless his body and speak life and healing over him. Then, I turn around and plug in his electric scooter. Love does not choose, and compassion does not quit. Love *is* a confrontation of suffering. Charles Kraft writes, "Jesus was not love one minute and power the next. He was both at all times. Jesus … used God's power always to demonstrate God's love. The purpose of spiritual power in Christianity is, then, to show love."[3]

Believers must "stick to" their commission to confront suffering. They must own this charge. Jesus' compassion is their commission. The weight and wonder of such a commission begs the question, "How are believers able to carry this?" What confidence do individuals have to continue Christ's commission to compassionately confront suffering? Believers do so just as Christ did—through the anointing of the Spirit.

---

3   Charles H. Kraft, *Christianity with Power: Your Worldview and Your Experience of the Supernatural* (Eugene, OR: Wipf and Stock Publishers, 1989), 123.

9

Our Confidence for the Commission

The Anointing of the Spirit for Compassionate Ministry

The weight of the Church's commission is great. The task to herald the good news of the Kingdom and confront suffering is beyond human capacity to fulfill. However, God does not leave believers ill equipped for their assignment. The promise of the Holy Spirit includes His anointing—His empowering presence—to do what Jesus sends them to do. Just as Jesus received anointing for His ministry, the Holy Spirit is present and is empowering believers to carry on the ministry of Christ to the afflicted.

Jesus and the Anointing of the Spirit

Jesus exercises His earthly ministry by the power of the Spirit. He does not open blind eyes, make the lame walk, and raise the dead by His divine status but by divine supply. Having willingly emptied himself of divine privilege, He takes on the form of a servant (Phil. 2:6-8), receiving and relying totally upon the Holy Spirit (John 1:32). C. Peter Wagner writes, "The Holy Spirit was the source of all Jesus' power during His earthly ministry. Jesus exercised no power of or by Himself."[1]

---

[1] C. Peter Wagner, *How to Have a Healing Ministry in Any Church: A Comprehensive Guide* (Ventura, CA: Regal Books, 1988), 114.

There is no record of any supernatural ministry exercised by Jesus prior to His baptism and the coming of the Spirit upon Him (Matt. 3:16). Gospel writers emphasize the significance of the "Spirit-event" and the events that follow in Jesus' life. Everything Jesus does after this event, He does because of and by the power of this experience.

Luke records that the Spirit comes upon Jesus after His baptism (Luke 3:21). He describes Jesus as "full of the Spirit" and being led into the wilderness (4:1). Jesus returns to Galilee in the "power of the Spirit," and the news regarding Jesus (presumably His ministry, as the context implies) spreads through the whole countryside (v. 14). Jesus goes to Nazareth, and on the Sabbath he stands in the synagogue, reading from Isaiah 61. The "Spirit of the Lord" is upon Him, which delineates the powerful, compassionate work the Spirit's anointing empowers Him to do, including freedom for prisoners, recovery of sight for the blind, freedom for the oppressed, and the announcing of God's favor (vv. 18-19). Perhaps more than any other writer, Luke makes it clear that Jesus' ministry is in and by the power of the Holy Spirit. Hendricksen notes, "This explanation of the source of Christ's power is the only logical one."[2]

Jesus acknowledges that He accomplishes these works by the power of the Spirit. In fact, it is the presence of the Spirit working upon and through Jesus that signals the presence of the kingdom of God. Jesus states, "But if it is by the Spirit of God that I drive out demons, then the kingdom of God has come upon you" (Matt. 12:28). Green recognizes that Jesus "attributes his acts of exorcism as a sign of the work of the Spirit in His mission, and as demonstration of God's kingdom at work."[3] Blomberg adds, "Jesus Himself claims that he exorcises the demon by power of the Holy Spirit, who descended on Him at His baptism, marking the inauguration of God's reign, and who permanently empowers all disciples for ministry in the messianic age."[4]

---

2 Hendricksen, 526.
3 Green, 538.
4 Blomberg, *Matthew*, 202.

The Anointing of the Spirit for Believers

Jesus promises the same anointing of the Holy Spirit to His followers. Luke cites this promise at the conclusion of his first volume when Jesus states that His disciples will be "clothed with power" (Luke 24:49). It appears again at the beginning of his second volume when Jesus promises believers, "You shall receive power" (Acts 1:8). In both references, Luke describes Jesus using the word *power* in reference to the consequence of receiving the promise of the Holy Spirit.

What did Luke mean by "power?" No small amount of ink has been spilled to assign meaning to Luke's quote. But the text will make it plain. Luke uses the word "power" often enough for readers to anticipate its meaning. Remembering that the gospel of Luke and the book of Acts share authorship, it is best to see where and how "power" was used prior to Acts 1:8. Luke uses the word *power* to refer to the working of the Spirit in the birth narratives of John the Baptist and Jesus (Luke 1:17, 1:35). Luke again uses this word in reference to the beginning of Christ's ministry (4:14). In Luke 4:36, the crowds recognize that with "power and authority" Jesus gives commands to "evil spirits and they come out." In Luke 5:17, Luke states that the power of the Lord was present with Jesus when He heals the sick. In Luke 6:19 and Luke 8:46, power literally flows out of Jesus, ministering healing to those who come in contact with Him. Regarding 6:19, Bock writes that the "text emphasizes the power that proceeds from him" and that this powerful ministry "reflects the compassion and love he claims God has for humanity."[5] Each time Luke has used the word "power" it refers directly to the active presence of the Holy Spirit, and most times it connotes the healing of disease or the driving out of demons.

Therefore, when Luke uses this same word to refer to the disciples' reception of the Holy Spirit (Acts 1:8), believers should anticipate that Jesus intends His followers to exercise the same compassionate power ministering to the ill and oppressed. C. Peter Wagner agrees, "We today can expect to do the same or greater things that Jesus did because we have been given access to the same

---

5   Bock, 120.

power source."[6] Stanley Horton asserts that this power "would be their [the followers of Jesus] secret of success in the Church Age until its final consummation when Jesus returns."[7] Bruce boldly asserts that, "As Jesus had been anointed at his baptism with the Holy Spirit and power, so his followers were now to be similarly anointed and enabled to carry on his work."[8]

The Pentecost event in Acts 2:4 initiates this anointing upon Christ's first followers, and the subsequent Spirit events fill them and countless others with the power of the Holy Spirit. Witherington recognizes the connection between the anointing upon Jesus and the anointing upon His followers. He argues that if the disciples are able to do the same works as Jesus, He does not perform miracles because of His divinity, or His followers would also be divine. Witherington continues, "Jesus derived his power and authority from the Spirit at His baptism and this same Spirit empowers his followers."[9] Norberto Saracco adds, "The power of the Spirit which a believer has is not inferior to the power which Jesus had. In the Kingdom, the power at work is one and the same."[10]

Believers' greatest confidence for ministry should rest in the Holy Spirit. Peter Wagner writes, "The Holy Spirit was the source of all Jesus' power during His earthly ministry. Jesus exercised no power of or by Himself. We today can expect to do the same or greater things that Jesus did because we have been given access to the same power source."[11] Wagner also affirms believers' confidence in the Spirit by saying, "The power that Jesus passed to His disciples did not arrive until the day of Pentecost. But when it did, it came to stay, and it provides the basis for ... doing the works of the Father through

---

6   Wagner, 114.

7   Stanley Horton, *The Book of Acts* (Springfield, MO: Gospel Publishing House, 1981), 22.

8   Bruce, 36.

9   Witherington, 218.

10   Norberto Saracco," The Holy Spirit and the Church's Mission of Healing," *International Review of Mission* 93 (July-October 2004), 416.

11   C. Peter Wagner, *How to Have a Healing Ministry in Any Church: A Comprehensive Guide* (Ventura, CA: Regal Books, 1988), 114.

the power brought by the Holy Spirit, just as Jesus did them."[12] James Shelton writes, "Luke makes it clear that Jesus also healed as a human empowered by the Holy Spirit. Luke uses identical terms to describe Spirit empowerment for both Jesus and his followers."[13]

Those who successfully minister healing attribute their successes to the work of the Holy Spirit. Carrie Judd Montgomery, a matriarch of healing ministry and healing homes in North America in the late 1800s, affirms that her confidence for healing was in the person and work of the Holy Spirit: "None who have felt the wonderful power, which, in answer to the prayer of faith, gives healing to soul and body, can doubt that it is the power of the Holy Spirit, promised to all ages and generations."[14] Kathryn Kuhlman writes that the key to healing is not the introspection or evaluation of one's faith,[15] but rather it is the Holy Spirit.[16] Describing the role of the Spirit in her meetings, Kuhlman says, "The presence of the Holy Spirit has been in such abundance that by His presence alone, sick bodies are healed, even as people wait outside the building for the doors to open."[17] Kuhlman is recognized for placing emphasis on the presence of the Holy Spirit in her ministry. Candy Gunther Brown notes:

> Kuhlman emphasized that the Holy Spirit was not an impersonal force, but the third person of the Trinity. God the Father and God the Son remained in heaven, while God the Holy Spirit lived on earth and could be invited to inhabit particular places, whether churches, auditoriums, or individual human bodies. Instead of praying for the

---

12 Wagner, 131.

13 James B., Shelton, "A Reply to Keith Warrington's Response to 'Jesus and Healing: Yesterday and Today'," *Journal of Pentecostal Theology*, 16, Issue 2 (April 2008): 115.

14 Carrie Judd Montgomery, *The Prayer of Faith* (1894; repr., Memphis, TN: Bottom of the Hill Publishing, 2011), 25.

15 Kathryn Kuhlman, *I Believe in Miracles*, rev. ed. (S. Plainfield, NJ: Bridge Publishing, 1992), 224.

16 Ibid., 227.

17 Kuhlman, 227.

sick to be healed, Kuhlman taught that people could be healed in their seats under the ministration of the Holy Spirit.[18]

Bosworth also attests to the Holy Spirit's aid to believers' confidence when he states, "Faith in God has a much stronger foundation and a much stronger helper—the Holy Spirit—than either doubt, sin or disease has. The Holy Spirit will free your mind of all doubt if you rely on Him to do it. Trust Him and keep your attention on the Word of God"[19]

Contemporary Christian leaders and scholars agree. Author and Pastor Jim Garlow invites those who minister healing to first welcome and honor the Holy Spirit: "Where the Holy Spirit is present, healing occurs."[20] Gordon Fee, when analyzing the confidence that the Apostle Paul has in the Spirit, offers, "He [Paul] would simply not have understood the presence of the Spirit that did not also include the such evidences of the Spirit's working that he termed 'powers' which we translate 'miracles.'"[21]

Jesus points His followers to the Spirit, to rely upon His leadership, fellowship and partnership (John 14:16; 16:13-15; Acts 1:8). Placing confidence in the Comforter is not a principle, but it is principal.

Rightly and firmly placed confidence is essential. Without it, one may never take the risks involved for ministering healing and deliverance. Also, appropriately placed confidence helps to ensure appropriately placed credit and praise. It was strong confidence in the nature and name of Jesus and the assuring presence of the Holy Spirit that moves Peter to grab the lame man at the beautiful gate by the hand and command him to rise up and walk. It is that same appropriately placed confidence that causes Peter to immediately

---

18 Candy Gunther Brown, "From Tent Meetings and Store-front Healing Rooms to Walmarts and the Internet: Healing Spaces in the United States, the Americas, and the World, 1906-2006," *Church History*, 75 no 3 (S 2006): 635.

19 Bosworth, 134.

20 James Garlow, *God Still Heals* (Indianapolis, IN: Wesleyan Publishing House, 2005), 209.

21 Gordon D. Fee, *Paul, the Spirit and the People of God* (Peabody, MA: Hendrickson, 1996), 166.

ask a wonder-filled crowd of on-lookers, "Why do you look at us as though by our own power or godliness we made this man walk? God has glorified His servant Jesus Christ" (Acts 3:1-13). Appropriately placed, sound confidence gives Christ's followers the liberty to minister without the encumbrance of seeking credit for the outcome.

The Holy Spirit is the all-sufficient source and supply for the believers' confidence to continue the compassionate confrontation of suffering. No aspect of the Kingdom—power, purity, proclamation or compassion—is possible apart from the Spirit. Frank Macchia makes the argument that the Spirit *is* the Kingdom. Macchia writes, "The Son is the King and the Spirit is the Kingdom in the fulfillment of the Father's will. Through Christ as the Spirit Baptizer, the Spirit brings creation into the kingdom of the King by indwelling all things with the divine presence so as to deliver creation from the reign of death unto the reign of life."[22] The believers' confidence is only and always in the sufficiency and supremacy of the Holy Spirit.

It is incumbent upon believers not only to faithfully receive the Spirit (to be-being filled with the Spirit – Eph. 5:18), but to cultivate an increasing consciousness of His abiding, empowering presence. A growing, confident awareness of the Holy Spirit will have multiplied benefits to a believer, not the least of which will be an increase in the exercise of the Sprit's power to confront suffering.

---

22 Frank D. Macchia, *Baptized in the Spirit: A Global Pentecostal Theology* (Grand Rapids, MI: Zondervan, 2006), 91.

Part Two

Common Sense Compassion: Everyday Approaches to Helping the Hurting

10

COMMAND, CONTACT AND CLIMATE

Believers, trusting in the power of the Holy Spirit, should emulate the same simplicity Jesus used when ministering to the ill or oppressed. This book asserts that practitioners have made too much of models and formulas with regard to ministering to the suffering, too often resulting in increased frustration or even greater harm. It is imperative that contemporary believers do not place their confidence in any series of steps or specific methods. Wagner rejects any notion of such a formula when he says, "There is no secret formula, ritual or procedure, which, when used correctly, makes the healing happen."[1] While believers should make every effort to avoid trust in formulas or methods, there are two basic biblical approaches for ministry to the suffering.

COMMAND AND CONTACT

For the purpose of this book and in order to suggest the simplest approach for ministry, these approaches will be *command* and *contact*. Several authors express agreement with this thought. Kraft notes these two common means, explaining that "we would not call what Jesus did when He ministered to

---

1 Wagner, 224.

people as 'prayer.' He usually commanded the condition to respond or the sick person to do something in faith. Or he would touch the person. Jesus prayed before his deeds, not during them."[2]

Jesus uses two primary means when dealing with the ill or oppressed. He speaks to, touches, or does both actions to the person in need. With authority, Jesus speaks and unclean spirits obey (Luke 4:36). With a touch, power leaves Him and brings healing (8:46). Jesus both speaks to and touches the leper (5:13). It may be that this is what Luke describes, when Jesus calls the twelve disciples together and gives them "power and authority over all demons and to cure diseases" (Luke 9:1). Power seems to correlate with contact, and authority with command. Jesus speaks (commands) with authority, and unclean spirits obey (4:36). With a touch (contact), power goes out from Jesus and brings healing (8:46). Jesus both speaks to and touches the leper (5:13).

Green offers this analysis—Jesus heals directly, exercising unmediated power to heal. He never asks God to intervene on behalf of the sick. Rather, he either pronounces healing directly or uses touch to heal. Green notes that "touch communicates and affirms the extension of God's own hand which acted in creation and deliverance in the OT, and so signifies the power of God at work."[3] Hendricksen observes, "A mere touch of the hand was all that was necessary, but what a power and what a sympathy there was in that touch."[4]

Whether the ministry is healing or exorcism, Jesus does not utilize complex approaches. Witherington notes that Jesus does not use the methodology of His day, which includes "rings, roots, incantations spells and the like," in His exorcisms.[5] Leon Morris observes that, "the mode of healing practiced by Jesus is infinitely simple, externally unimpressive, but inwardly so much more powerful."[6]

Howard Ervin invests the most into explaining and emphasizing command as means of communicating a cure. He explains an Old Testament

---

2   Kraft, 124.
3   Green, 536.
4   Hendricksen, 400.
5   Witherington, 193.
6   Morris, 88.

view that a word, once spoken, "carries with it something of the life force of the speaker. It assumes an independent existence."[7] Commenting on John 4:50, Ervin illustrates this point: "Jesus' words released a creative energy that initiated healing even as the words were spoken."[8] Ervin then exemplifies the use of touch in the ministry of Jesus—stating when it occurs, its results, and the Old Testament prophetic allusions therein.[9] It may be helpful to note that literature does not suggest that healing and deliverance result from specific words or any certain touches. There is no formula for these ministries.

Contemporary believers should have confidence that there is far more at work than empty words or symbolic touches.

CLIMATE

In ministry, climate is as important as confidence. Even with the correct infrastructure present and the proper doctrines and methods in place, ministry will suffer if the climate is unhelpful. Love creates the most conducive climate for healing and deliverance. In fact, love is the sole measure of the success of ministries. Paul makes this clear in 1 Corinthians 13:1-3 when he argues that apart from love, no ministry expression has real value or lasting benefit. Literature presents a strong case for fostering a climate of love when ministering healing and deliverance.

Ervin makes the case for love's efficacy in ministry, explaining that "if faith heals, and it does, so also does love."[10] This exemplifies the truth from Luke 7:50, where Jesus says that the woman living in sin "has loved much" and then says to her, "your faith has saved you."[11] MacNutt also equates the value of love with faith when he writes, "While faith is helpful for healing, both in the sick person and in the one praying for a healing, the primary disposition

---

7   Ervin, 34.
8   Ibid., 35.
9   Ervin, 45-54. Ervin walks the reader through several miracle stories where Jesus touches the person in need, affecting a cure.
10 Ervin, 18.
11 Ibid.

needed in the minister of healing is love."[12] In fact, MacNutt testifies that he has witnessed healing, "especially" when in loving communities.[13] Mary Ann McColl and Richard S. Ascough claim that the scriptural accounts of healing carry an intrinsic, loving message to the afflicted: "From the perspective of those who work alongside people with disabilities and provide care or service, the healing miracles in the gospels consistently evoke themes of inclusiveness, advocacy and courage."[14]

Further, literature affirms the synonymous relationship between power and love. Kraft writes, "Jesus was not love one minute and power the next. He was both at all times. Jesus ... used God's power always to demonstrate God's love. The purpose of spiritual power in Christianity is, then, to show love."[15] Kraft writes further: "As with Jesus so with us; God's power comes wrapped in God's love."[16] John Wimber also affirms this relationship, explaining, "Jesus is the God of love, and He is the God of power ... Jesus' use of power was integral to his message of love ... In Jesus, love and power are inseparable."[17] Wimber goes on to make this absolute statement: "Spiritual power for the Christian always demonstrates God's love."[18] MacNutt concurs: "In the healing ministry, one can concentrate on either of two attributes: the power of God or the Love of God. Healing is a manifestation of both. Emphasize love."[19]

A climate of love ensures a positive outcome, regardless of whether or not believers observe miracles. Wagner explains how this is true: "Praying for the sick, when motivated and ministered by love is always a win–because we've partnered with the Holy Spirit to touch someone in a meaningful way.

---

12   MacNutt, *Healing*, 119.

13   Ibid., 11.

14   Mary Ann McColl and Richard S. Ascough, "Jesus and People with Disabilities: Old Stories, New Approaches," *Journal of Pastoral Care & Counseling*, 63 no 3-4 (Fall/Winter 2009): 8.

15   Charles H. Kraft, *Christianity with Power: Your Worldview and Your Experience of the Supernatural* (Eugene, OR: Wipf and Stock Publishers, 1989), 123.

16   Ibid.

17   Wimber, *Power Evangelism*, 153.

18   Ibid., 154.

19   MacNutt, *Healing*, 121.

It is rare that this expression will ever leave someone resentful or regretful."[20] David Lim makes the same argument in reverse: "ministry apart from love brings negative results."[21]

Believers should practice deliverance in the same climate as healing. Hammond writes that Christians can perform deliverance in a "relaxed atmosphere without tension or put-upon drama."[22] Pablo Bottari insists that love drives deliverance, explaining that "you aren't trying to cast out a demon, but help someone who the Lord loves and does not want to hurt."[23] Kris Valloton agrees, "The person's dignity should be our priority during any session. I always try to make people feel safe and loved as we work to get them free."[24]

Richard Foster summarizes the need for and benefit of ministering in love, explaining that love makes healing and deliverancee a normal expression of the nature of God exercised by those willing, not just celebrities: "When we see divine healing as simply part of the normal life of the people of God, we are freed from elevating one ministry above another. Seen in this light, healing prayer is merely a way of showing love to people in need. Healing–physical and otherwise–is the natural outflow of compassion, God's and ours."[25] Agnes Sanford celebrates the climate of love:

> What, then, is Christian love? Christian love is the love of Christ, an energy so overwhelming that it led our Lord to give His life for His friends, and to give it away with a joy that carried Him through untold anguish. Christian love is a powerful, radiant and life-giving

---

20 Wagner, 212.
21 David Lim, *Spiritual Gifts: A Fresh Look* (Springfield, MO: Gospel Publishing House, 1991), 113.
22 Hammond, 84.
23 Pablo Deiros and Pablo Bottari, "Deliverance from Dark Strongholds," in *Power, Holiness and Evangelism Rediscovering God's Purity, Power and Passion for the Lost*, ed. Randy Clark (Shippensburg, PA: Destiny Image, 1999), 112.
24 Kris Valloton, *Spirit Wars: Winning the Invisible Battle Against Sin and the Enemy* (Minneapolis, MN: Chosen Books, 2012), 178.
25 Richard Foster, "Introduction" in *Power Healing* by John Wimber and Kevin Springer (New York: HarperCollins, 1987), xi.

emotion, charged with healing power both to the one who learns to love and the one who is loved.[26]

Emphasizing love as the climate for ministry provides a strong contrast to the sometimes-condemning tones that insist that either the needy or the ministers must conjure up sufficient faith to gain a response from heaven. Fostering a climate of love is not only refreshing but also required. It does not replace faith with feeling; instead it energizes and accesses faith by love. Paul writes that the only thing that counts is faith, which works by love (Gal. 5:6).

---

26 Agnes Sanford, *The Healing Light* (New York: Random House, 1947), 51.

11

APPROACHING HEALING

SEVERAL AUTHORS SUGGEST step-by-step models believers should use when ministering healing. None of these authors imply that the steps they prescribe are formulas or equations that guarantee results; nor do the authors insist that Christians must apply their specific models to affect cures. These authors present models based on their observations and reflections of biblical data, their experiences, the testimonies of others, and common sense application of this information. Sanford suggests four steps to prayer,[1] while Alexander Venter lays out a step-by-step approach.[2] Kraft and Wimber describe five steps.[3] This chapter synthesizes their recommendations below.

INVITE:

Recalling the confidence believers should place in the person and work of the Spirit, it is healthy and helpful to pause to acknowledge and welcome the Spirit's immediate presence and influence. This is not to say the Spirit is distant unless invoked, but turning the focus to His presence is an appropriate

---

1   Sanford, 52.
2   Alexander Venter, *Doing Healing: How to Minister God's Kingdom in the Power of the Spirit* (Cape Town, South Africa: Vineyard International Publishing, 2009), 264-265.
3   Kraft, 155; Garlow, 219-223.

act of worship, and it turns attention away from those praying and helps place the problems in perspective.

Sanford invests much effort into this aspect of ministering healing, introducing the idea early and emphasizing it throughout her text.[4] She encourages the individuals praying and those in need of prayer to relax and meditate on the reality of God's presence. In this relaxed state, those praying should ask for the indwelling of God's life and give thanks for the increase of His power within His followers. When Wimber ministers, he encourages people to "dial down," or relax and resist becoming worked up emotionally. He writes, "Stirred up emotions rarely aid the healing process."[5]

Kraft and Venter both suggest that ministry begin by inviting the Spirit to participate and include "blessing" those receiving the ministry. Venter refers to this as "blessing the person with Christ's healing presence," and includes the simple prayer, "Come, Holy Spirit."[6]

ASK

Kraft, Garlow, and Wimber recommend pausing to interview the person in need.[7] For example, they suggest the minister ask about the nature of the problem, the location of the pain, the start of the problem, and any other relevant issues that can be conversed about briefly. Garlow explains, "Prayers are more effective when we zero in on the problem."[8] One may find it curious to interview others regarding the nature of their problems after inviting the Spirit and blessing those receiving the prayers. Why not determine the problem first? One could argue that focusing first on God's presence and expressing His loving presence with a blessing helps to provide the perfect backdrop and climate of loving confidence to address the pressing needs of those in pain.

---

4   Sanford, 52.
5   Wimber, *Power Healing*, 174.
6   Kraft, 155, Venter, 264.
7   Kraft, 155, Garlow, 219.
8   Garlow, 219.

Garlow continues to explain that interviews may help to diagnose the problems. Kraft calls this the tentative diagnosis.[9] Garlow encourages the ministers to ask questions that will uncover any important issues beyond the physical symptoms presented. For example, ministers can ask, "Is this an inner problem? Is this stress? How are the person's relationships? What is going on in their lives right now?"[10] He adds, importantly, "Remember, this is not an interrogation. We're motivated by love, not merely a desire to know the details of a person's life. During this interview, be asking, 'Holy Spirit, show us how to pray.'"[11]

The person's pain may be more emotional, which can exacerbate or cause their physical pain. According to Don Colbert, inner problems, or issues in people's emotional lives, can contribute negatively to individuals' physical health. Therefore, leaders should consider emotional well-being when ministering healing. Colbert informs, "Certain emotions release hormones into the physical body that, in turn, can trigger the development of a host of diseases."[12] Because of neuropeptides, if people's brains interpret physical perceptions like anger, fear or depression, every immune cell in their bodies know that interpretation very quickly. In turn, Colbert explains that fear triggers "more than fourteen hundred known physical and chemical stress reactions and activates more than thirty different hormones and neurotransmitters."[13] The emotions most physically damaging include unforgiveness, depression, anger, worry, frustration, fear, grief, and guilt.[14] Colbert argues that one of the worst things individuals can "feel" in their hearts is hostility, or a general cynical worldview.[15]

---

9   Kraft, 155.
10   Ibid., 220.
11   Ibid., 221.
12   Don Colbert, *Deadly Emotions: Understand the Mind-Body-Spirit Connection that Can Heal or Destroy You* (Nashville, TN: Thomas Nelson, 2003), xi.
13   Colbert, 13.
14   Ibid., 20.
15   Ibid., 35.

Therefore, the interview process should help ministers understand whether the people need "inner" healing. While this term may carry the baggage of controversy, it should not. Carlos Mraida explains that inner healing simply "confronts people with the love and power of God and leads them to find freedom from inner strongholds that previously impeded living as God desires."[16]

ACT

After an interview and "diagnosis," leaders should minister to the people's needs directly. Venter recommends the laying on of hands at this point.[17] Kraft recommends engaging in a tentative prayer strategy, meaning that the ministers should determine what "kind" of prayer the individuals need.[18]

Garlow explains that prayers may take several different forms, including "petition, intercession, command, rebuke, or pronouncement."[19] Petition is a simple request for God to intervene in the moment. Intercession means that the ministers may need to devote themselves to longer-term prayer-partnerships on behalf of the people in need. When discussing command, Garlow asserts the Holy Spirit may prompt ministers to speak to specific issues, usually demonic influences or strongholds, in Jesus' name. A rebuke is similar, used under the direction of the Holy Spirit when ministers believe "demonic affliction or direct involvement of the enemy" creates the problems for those in need.[20] During intervention, Venter encourages ministers to watch and work with God, to observe what is happening, and to bless what God is doing.[21] Sanford adds that the word "amen" at the end of prayer interventions serve

---

16 Carlos Mraida, "Inner Healing to Live in Freedom," in *Power, Holiness and Evangelism Rediscovering God's Purity, Power and Passion for the Lost Deliverance from Dark Strongholds*, ed. Randy Clark (Shippensburg, PA: Destiny Image, 1999), 101-102.
17 Venter, 264.
18 Kraft, 155.
19 Garlow, 221-222.
20 Ibid.
21 Venter, 265.

as "a command sent forth in the name of Christ."[22] Sanford also urges ministers to do all of the above with joy, because "prayer needs wings of joy to fly upon."[23]

ASK AGAIN, ACT AGAIN

After prayer, ministers should pause and evaluate the conditions of the people, determining if they see any changes. Venter suggests getting feedback at this point by having the individuals test it out and then address any blockage if possible.[24] If after checking for results there is no change, or if there is only some change, Garlow recommends praying again and asking better questions.[25] He encourages people to seek honest answers to questions like, "Is the condition or pain better, worse, or no different?"[26]

If people do not receive healing, or if their sicknesses return, Venter suggests that the individuals have not resolved some of the underlying conditions.[27] Garlow encourages ministers to keep praying by urging, "As long as God is working, you keep working."[28] Venter reminds that healing is warfare.[29] MacNutt notes that an extended time of prayer and remaining in yielded awareness of God's presence is often very helpful. He states, "One of the greatest discoveries of my life has been that when a short prayer doesn't seem to help, a 'soaking' prayer often brings the healing we are looking for."[30]

---

22 Sanford, 52.
23 Ibid., 57.
24 Venter, 265.
25 Garlow, 223.
26 Ibid.
27 Venter, 266.
28 Garlow, 223.
29 Venter, 266.
30 Francis MacNutt, *The Prayer that Heals: Praying for Healing in the Family* (Notre Dame, IN: Ave Maria Press, 1981), 57.

DIRECTION

Following prayer, Garlow recommends providing some after-care direction for the people. He cites Jesus' encouragement of a newly-raised-girl's parents to "give her something to eat" (Luke 8:55) Specifically, he mentions encouraging people to get rest and care for themselves, as well as address sinful or destructive behaviors that may lead to the conditions.[31]

Bosworth adds that the same posture of "relaxing" that is appropriate as people seek healing is appropriate as they wait for healing. Bosworth writes, "In receiving supernatural healing, the first thing to learn is to cease to be anxious about the condition of the body. You have committed it to the Lord and He has taken the responsibility for your healing. You are to be happy and restful in the matter. You know from His own Word that He takes the responsibility of every case committed Him."[32]

Finally, it is important to restate that the approaches above are not formulas, but helpful guides to effective ministry. Wagner rejects any notion of formulas for healing when he states, "There is no secret formula, ritual or procedure, which, when used correctly, makes the healing happen."[33]

Much of the literature concerning the ministry of healing argues that the practice is about common sense more than complex principles. Those engaging in healing interventions should avoid focusing on specific formulas or methods. Instead, they may follow common sense steps of treating people with honor, acknowledging specific problems and their potential sources, pausing to examine changes or improvements and continuing prayer. Above all, ministers must do everything to communicate love for those in need.

Every single person who has prayed for healing has experienced disappointment, even heartache. Our commitment to the commission is addressed earlier in this text. Kraft summarizes, "I made a decision. If God was going to participate in making people well, I would simply 'go for it.' I would pray for everybody he brought my way."[34]

---

31 Garlow, 224.
32 Bosworth, 131.
33 Wagner, 224.
34 Kraft, 79.

12

Approaching Deliverance

To cultivate confidence regarding the ministry of deliverance, it is important to answer a few introductory questions. What are demons and do they really exist? How do they gain access to their victims? How do they evince themselves? And finally, how should believers minister to those afflicted by demons?

Demons: Who They Are and How They Get In

Not everyone believes that demons exist, even in religious communities. MacNutt points out that the opinion of mainline theologians and commentators is "that demon possession and exorcism come out of a primitive, superstitious worldview that we have fortunately escaped, but which Jesus, a man of His day, accepted."[1] MacNutt argues that the primary reason people rule out the influence of the demonic world as a possible explanation for strange behavior and speech is "scientific rationalism, the predominant worldview since the so-called enlightenment."[2] While some reject the reality of any demonic

---

1   MacNutt, *Deliverance*, 47.
2   Ibid., 54.

presence, others seem to exhibit belief that borders on obsession. The majority of the surveyed literature affirms the existence of demons and offers explanations for how demons affect people's lives. L. Stafford Betty persuades the modern reader to recognize the real threat of demonic activity: "The fact that they do not discriminate, that their passions and machinations are as prevalent in India and China as in the Christian (or post-Christian) West, that they work their mischief all over the world makes us take them more seriously."[3]

Burkholder argues for the reality of the demonic realm when he writes, "Evil spirits are not relics of a magical, superstitious, pre-modern worldview, but real, evil, supernatural germs which need to be cleansed from their human carriers by the loving, restoring, powerful healing of the Lord Jesus Christ … Deliverance [is simply] the healing prayer and counseling means by which evil spirits are expelled from the individuals so plagued."[4]

Keith Warrington agrees, claiming that the New Testament summary of demons "shows that they are real, unclean, hostile, and powerful."[5] Dale Martin questions the traditional view that demons are fallen angels, arguing that we do not see in the NT demons equated with fallen angels.[6] Ervin offers a more detailed definition and description of demons as "independent beings who occupy a position somewhere between the human and the divine."[7]

Believers often refer to demons as unclean spirits. Peter Horrobin writes that the phrases "demons" and "evil or unclean spirits" appear to share the same meaning to the Gospel writers, who describe these entities as having similar effects in the lives of the demonized. He notes, "In general … it is assumed that when we are talking about deliverance ministry, we are dealing

---

[3] L. Stafford Betty, "The Growing Evidence for 'Demonic Possession': What Should Psychiatry's Response Be?" *Journal of Religion and Health*, 44 no 1 (Spring 2005): 20.

[4] Burkholder, 43.

[5] Keith Warrington, "Reflections on the History and Development of Demonological Beliefs and Praxis among British Pentecostals," *Asian Journal of Pentecostal Studies* 7:2 (2004): 283.

[6] Dale Basil Martin, "When Did Angels Become Demons?" *Journal of Biblical Literature*, 129, Issue 4 (Winter 2010): 675.

[7] Ervin, 55.

with spiritual powers in the service of Satan, generally called demons or evil spirits."[8] Ervin offers some analysis on this term. He states, "From the LXX, the word 'unclean' is used to characterize those things that could not be offered to God in worship, hence, anything offensive to the holiness of God. In a moral sense, it means that which is morally, 'unclean, impure, [and] vicious.' … [therefore,] The meaning of the word gives some insight into the nature of the creature so described."[9]

It is also helpful to understand that the term "possession" is not as accurate as the word "demonized." Prince explains that the verb *daimonizo* means people are subject to demonic influence, not possessed.[10] When seeking to explain how demons gain access to their victims, literature leans upon the anecdotal experiences and observations of authors. Because of this, much of the material is speculative, even if credible authors offer it. Warrington summarizes this problem when he writes, "The lack of biblical support for much that has been written makes the practice of exorcism subjective and even suspect, leaving a trail of speculation and confusion."[11]

The testimonies of the authors show that demons do not play fair or nice, and the realities of demonic oppression are serious and sad. Prince claims that demons gain access to their victims at "the weakest moment and the weakest place" in their lives.[12] Neal Lozano offers a list of access points, which includes trauma,[13] involvement in the occult,[14] self-inflicted curses, associations, environment, willful sins, or family sins.[15] Burkholder suggests that demons gain access through volitional and non-volitional doorways, or "cracks" in the

---

8   Peter Horrobin, *Healing Through Deliverance*, vol. 1 of *The Foundation of Deliverance Ministry* (Grand Rapids, MI: Chosen Books. 1991), 81.
9   Ervin, 57.
10 Prince, 16.
11 Warrington, 284.
12 Prince, 103.
13 Neal Lozano, *Unbound: A Practical Guide to Deliverance* (Grand Rapids, MI: Chosen Books, 2003), 42.
14 Ibid., 44.
15 Ibid., 47.

self.[16] When explaining these cracks, he states, "Volitional entry points depend on the fact that in some way the invaded person has made choices which give permission for demonic ingress. Non-volitional doorways are defined as afflictions in which the sufferer is victimized in some sense by demonic attachments over which (s)he has had little if any control."[17]

DEMONS: HOW THEY EVINCE THEMSELVES

In Scripture, particularly the passages concerning the ministry of Jesus, readers find that Jesus casts out demons—without explanation or description. Frederick J Gaiser says it succinctly, "In the Bible, demons are for driving out."[18] When people read specific encounters, demonized individuals seem to respond or manifest in manners that plainly show the gospel writers and the immediate audience that there are demons present. Today, with the infiltration of science fiction, horror films, and personal melodrama, it can be difficult for believers to determine when, if at all, they are dealing with demonized people.[19] Through their own experience and observations, some authors attempt to provide guidelines to determine the presence of demonic forces.

MacNutt writes, "In terms of 'is this a demonic affliction or just an emotional/psychological problem' the answer is usually 'both-and' and not 'either-or.'"[20] He describes what he believes to be evidences of demonic behavior, which he claims is cross-culturally and trans-geographically similar.[21] MacNutt suggests that when people suffer from demonization, they may exhibit behavior that is excessively and noticeably aberrant from their norm.

---

16 Burkholder, 44.
17 Ibid. See also Lozano, 42-47 for his listing of "common points of entry."
18 Frederick J. Gaiser, "Healing in the Bible: A Grateful Response," *Journal of Pentecostal Theology*, 21, Issue 1 (April 2012): 57.
19 This is not to suggest that I doubt the existence of the demonized. In fact, I believe the problem is far greater than the North American Evangelical church accepts. But superstition, suspicion, and immaturity have contributed to a general reluctance to even broach the subject.
20 MacNutt, *Deliverance*, 79.
21 Ibid., 25.

Demons may give rise to spontaneous hysterical outbursts. Demonized people might use first person plural pronouns, such as "we" and "our," instead of usual singular personal pronouns. They could become violent or make threats. There may be unusual physical manifestations, including unlearned behaviors. MacNutt acknowledges that physical manifestations are also sometimes responses to the Holy Spirit, but demons may even attempt to imitate behaviors normally attributed as such. However, MacNutt warns that demonic behavior is conspicuous and bears different fruit than that of the Holy Spirit, as well as immediate intent.[22] He claims believers may observe some other common symptoms of demonization.[23] Typically, the strongest signs of demon presence are bodily contortions, changes in voices, and changes in facial expressions. Believers may notice rigidity, especially around fingers. Facial changes are the most common, possibly portraying mockery, hate, or pride.[24] Further clues include unpleasant smells and above all, according to MacNutt, cold.[25]

Prince recognizes that demons remain invisible, but Christians can observe them by their effects.[26] He provides a summary of his observations of typical demonic activities. Prince says demons will entice, harass, and torture their victims. This might include physical pain (in the form of afflictions, illnesses and pains of varied sorts),[27] mental torment, or inner accusation (as constant, nagging, and random shame and fear which induces inner dialogue).[28] Prince also asserts that demons compel, causing compulsive behaviors and

---

22 Ibid.
23 Ibid., 81.
24 Ibid., 82.
25 Ibid., 83.
26 Prince, 165.
27 Horribin writes that "While not all sickness is demonic, there are far more demonically induced symptoms than the church would readily admit. And one of the main reasons why some people are not healed is that the demonic dimension is not being discerned, even by those who believe in and use the gifts of the Holy Spirit" (Horribin, 140).
28 Prince, 166-167.

some addictions.[29] He says demons may compel people to engage in behaviors that satisfy the demonic forces within."[30]

PROTECTING THE VICTIM

Ministers should not approach a demonized person with superstition or condemnation. Jacques Theron warns, "A problem is that paranoia breeds fear, a fascinated fearfulness in the dramatic details of how demons enter human beings."[31] Ministers must also avoid projecting any shame on the victims in any way. Warrington reminds that "Christ never treated the oppressed as morally responsible for their condition."[32] Even monitoring the vernacular that leaders use in deliverance ministry is helpful, if not necessary. Instead of using dramatic or shocking terms to describe their ministry, MacNutt suggests that ministers should refer to it as "praying to liberate people from the oppression of evil spirits."[33] Whether or not leaders use that specific language, the point is to use language that does not frighten or dishonor the victims.

HELPING THE VICTIM

Almost all of the literature concerning the actual methods of deliverance is experience-driven. The more specific the directions, the more the author's observations and personal testimonies influence those directions. The various authors' methods are not dissimilar. They share fundamental principles and patterns. Regarding methods, Hammond offers this strong caution: "There is a tendency to look for formulas instead of reliance upon the Holy Spirit. If we get success through a technique, we are prone to trust in that technique—as

---

29   Ibid., 169.
30   Ibid., 172.
31   Jacques Theron, "A Critical Overview of the Church's Ministry of Deliverance from Evil Spirits," *Pneuma: The Journal of the Society for Pentecostal Studies* 18:1 (Spring 1996): 81.
32   Warrington, 286.
33   MacNutt, *Deliverance*, 72.

if that is what did the trick. If we start looking for methods and techniques, we'll end up in 'hopeless confusion.'"[34] Those who minister must seek to learn from the wisdom of these authors' experiences but reject the temptation to place confidence anywhere other than the Comforter.

---

[34] Hammond, 77.

13

General Principles for Deliverance

Invite

As with ministering healing, always begin by welcoming and honoring the Holy Spirit. When seeking to minister deliverance, MacNutt first recommends that ministers pray for protection.[1] Also, he advises to use a team if possible, because teams help prevent scandal and allow for members of the team to rest if necessary. (MacNutt has often engaged in long-term deliverance sessions.) Teams also provide the support to physically restrain the victims if necessary, which is not uncommon in MacNutt's experiences. On a more positive note, teams may bring a variety of spiritual gifts to bear upon the interventions.[2]

Ask:

Next, leaders should interview the person needing ministry. They should ask the following questions: (1) Is there anything the person has done to contribute to the situation? (2) Is the person a victim of sin (rape, incest, abuse, etc.)? and (3) When did this start?[3] MacNutt believes it is important to identify

---

1   MacNutt, *Deliverance,* 170.
2   Ibid, 154-157.
3   Ibid., 159-160.

the types of spirits tormenting the individuals. This is a common discussion among deliverance practitioners. Not all scholars insist on it, and some even reject the necessity outright. However, those who argue in favor of it, like MacNutt, reason strongly that using a spirit's name gives leverage over the specific spirits and may shed light on the means by which the spirits gain access to the victims.[4]

ACT:

When expelling an evil spirit, MacNutt reminds ministers that the deliverance prayer is not actually a prayer but a command. Leaders should speak directly to the tormenting spirit, using the Name of Jesus, telling the spirit to depart.[5] He offers some suggestions along these lines, reminding the practitioner to be compassionate, to speak calmly, and to look people in the eyes.[6]

When attempting to determine if spirits have left the victims, MacNutt notes that process is ultimately a matter of discernment—of both the team ministering and the victim. The victim will generally feel relief, lightness, and joy. MacNutt acknowledges the team may feel quite weary.[7] Finally, he instructs the ministers and former victims to "fill the emptiness" by praying for the Holy Spirit's infilling.[8]

WHEN DEMONS DEPART

When demons depart, their departures may range from unnoticeable to dramatic. A few notes from authors' observations may prove intriguing and perhaps beneficial. Readers should note that the following has anecdotal roots, but some similarities are present in Scripture. Prince suggests that demons

---

4   Ibid., 161.
5   Ibid., 169.
6   Ibid., 171-172.
7   MacNutt, *Deliverance*, 177.
8   Ibid., 180.

actually leave one's body in different ways, but especially from the mouth.⁹ This leads him to counsel victims to "blow it out" and keep blowing while keeping the path clear of other expressions from the mouth, including groaning, roaring, loud crying, coughing, yawning, etc. At first this testimony may seem excessive. But in Gospel narratives, when demons leave their victims, it is often with some sort of loud cry (Luke 4:33, 41). Hammond also affirms that demons leave primarily via the mouth or nose.¹⁰ He says, "Undoubtedly the most common manifestation is coughing."¹¹ In other cases, victims may even vomit, with mucus or phlegm, sometimes in large amounts, coming out. Even after meals, it is rare for actual food to come out. Sometimes for an hour this will occur.¹²

Advising ministers on how to approach deliverance is difficult, and the material authors present on this area of discussion is hard to process. The more authors press details, the more potential for superstition and paranoia presents itself. There are many anecdotal stories of long-fought exorcisms and haunting claims of multiple demonic points-of-entry. Believers may feel uneasy regarding the details of the authors' testimonies, However, they must acknowledge that the authors' general theses that demonic oppression and harassment is far more prevalent than modern leaders commonly acknowledge appears to be accurate. Their testimonies invite a fresh reading of the Gospel accounts, recognizing the widespread infestation of the demonic realm and the militant expulsion thereof as the kingdom of God arrives in Christ Jesus.

---

9   Ibid., 205.
10 Hammond, 51.
11 Ibid., 52.
12 Ibid.

14

Conclusion

People are hurting everywhere, in and out of church. Jesus still sees the world's masses and feels compassion toward them. He still sees them as harassed and helpless, and His solution for their suffering has not changed. He still calls His followers to himself, anointing them and sending them out to herald the good news of forgiveness of sin and reconciliation to God through faith in Christ. He sends them to powerfully and compassionately confront suffering.

Using key biblical passages, this book sought to provide a biblical-theological basis for this confidence by demonstrating the source and supply of this assurance in (1) the nature and mission of the kingdom of God, (2) the commission of the Church, and (3) the anointing of the Holy Spirit.

Contemporary believers should have confidence that the nature and mission of the kingdom of God has not changed. God's nature is good; His redeeming mission is compassionate. They should believe that Christ's compassion is also their commission. They may have confidence in the anointing of the Holy Spirit, the same Spirit who empowers and enabled Jesus to help the hurting and oppressed. They should use the loving power of words and touch to express the authority and power of the Holy Spirit. Believers should not surrender to suffering in the face of discouragement or failure. Love always hopes, and love never fails.

15

God Hates Suffering

Suffering can and should be fought on every front. God hates the suffering of those who hurt. God hates the suffering of those under torment. God hates the suffering of the teenage girl who struggles to feel loved and lovely. God hates the suffering of young men who have had their identities robed. God hates the suffering of the drug addict, the shame of the felon, the weight of depression, the ache of loneliness. God hates the suffering of children who are without home and without hope, or who cannot run and play because their little bodies do not work right. God has compassion on the suffering. His compassion is powerful. And His compassion is our commission.

What you believe God feels about suffering will influence how you feel. What He has done about it will inspire you to do something about it.

The kingdom of God is at hand. God has reconciled humankind to himself in Christ by making Him who knew no sin to become sin so that people might become the righteousness of God (2 Cor. 5:21). Believers will preach repentance for the forgiveness of sin in His name to all nations (Luke 24:47). The gospel is a proclamation of unspeakable good news—there is forgiveness of sin and restoration to right relationship with God. Because believers are His children, He gives them the Spirit of His Son in their hearts (Gal. 4:6). The preaching of the gospel is a proclamation of the unsearchable riches of Christ—of all that God is for humankind and has done for them in Christ.

Concurrent to this proclamation is the mandate to powerfully confront suffering in every form. People, both in and out of the Church, are hurting. Jesus models a ministry of compassion that confronts illness and oppression, and He commissions His church to continue His ministry. The Holy Spirit anoints believers to carry on this commission.

Ministry to the sick and afflicted should be normal expressions of the love of God in Christ. Love *is* a confrontation of suffering. Love does not have to choose between natural and supernatural means of ministering to the afflicted, but believers can and should use every means available to confront suffering at every level.

Christ-followers should have confidence to follow the footsteps of Christ, the One who "went about doing good and healing all who were oppressed of the devil" (Acts 10:38). This book purposed to gather and present biblical and theological reasons for this confidence. It is my hope that this book will contribute to a larger movement of confident compassion in the Church at large.

"Your Kingdom come; Your will be done; As in Heaven – so on earth."

Sources Consulted

Blomberg, Craig. *Matthew*. The New American Commentary. Nashville, TN: Broadman, 1992.

Blomberg, Craig, and Mariam J. Kamell. "James." *Exegetical Commentary on the New Testament*. Grand Rapids, MI: Zondervan, 2008.

Bock Darrel L. *Luke*. The IVP New Testament Commentary Series. Downers Grove, IL: InterVarsity Press, 1994.

Bruce, F. F. *Acts*. New International Commentary on the New Testament. Grand Rapids, MI: Eerdmans, 1988.

Bruner, Frederick Dale. *The Christ Book: Matthew 1-12*. Vol. 1 of *Matthew*. Grand Rapids, MI: Eerdmans, 2004.

Burkholder Lawrence. "The Theological Foundations of Deliverance Healing." *Conrad Grebel Review* 19, no. 1 (Winter 2001): 38-68.

Dodd, C. H. "Miracles in the Gospels." *Expository Times* 44 (1932-33): 504-509.

Ervin Howard M. *Healing: Sign of the Kingdom*. Peabody, MA: Hendrickson Publishers, 2002.

Evans, Craig. *Matthew*. New Cambridge Bible Commentary. New York: Cambridge University Press, 2012.

Fee, Gordon D. *Paul, the Spirit and the People of God*. Peabody, MA: Hendrickson, 1996.

France, R. T. *The Gospel of Matthew*. The New International Commentary on the New Testament. Grand Rapids, MI: Eerdmans, 2007.

Garlow James, *God Still Heals: Answers to Your Questions about Divine Healing* Indianapolis, IN: Wesleyan Publishing House, 2005.

Gerhardsson, Biger. *The Mighty Acts of Jesus According to Matthew*. Lund, Sweden: CWK Gleerup, 1979.

Green, Joel B. "Healing." In *The New Dictionary of Biblical Theology*, edited by T. Desmond Alexander, Brian Rosner, D. A. Carson, and Graeme Goldsworthy, 536-540. Downers Grove, IL: InterVarsity, 2000.

Hansen G. Walter. Galatians. *The IVP Testament Commentary Series*. Downers Grove, IL: InterVarsity Press, 1994.

Harris, M. J. "Salvation." In *The New Dictionary of Biblical Theology*, edited by T. Desmond Alexander, Brian Rosner, D. A. Carson, and Graeme Goldsworthy 762-767. Downers Grove, IL: InterVarsity, 2000.

Hendricksen, William. *The Gospel of Matthew*. The New Testament Commentary, Edinburgh: Banner of Truth, 1973.

Horton, Stanley. *Acts*. Logion Press Commentary. Springfield, MO: Logion, 1981.

Hughes Philip E. *The Second Epistle to the Corinthians*. The New International Commentary on the New Testament. Grand Rapids, MI: Eerdmans, 1962.

Kee, Howard Clark. "Medicine and Healing." In *The Anchor Bible Dictionary*, edited by David Noel Freedman, 659-664. New York: Doubleday, 1992.

Keener, Craig S. *A Commentary on the Gospel of Matthew*. Grand Rapids, MI: Eerdmans, 1999.

Kistemaker, Simon. *Exposition of the Acts of the Apostles*. New Testament Commentary. Grand Rapids, MI: Baker, 1990.

Kuemmerline-McLean, Joanne K. "Demons." In *Anchor Bible Dictionary*, edited by David Noel Freedman, 138-140. New York: Doubleday, 1992.

Larkin William J., Jr. *Acts*. The IVP New Testament Commentary Series. Downers Grove, IL: InterVarsity, 1995.

Liefeld Walter L. *Luke*. The Expositor's Bible Commentary. Grand Rapids, MI: Zondervan, 1984.

Macchia Frank D. *Baptized in the Spirit: A Global Pentecostal Theology*. Grand Rapids, MI: Zondervan, 2006.

Marshal, I. Howard. *1 Peter*. The IVP New Testament Commentary Series. Downers Grove, IL: InterVarsity Press, 1991.

Morris, Leon. "Matthew." *The Pillar New Testament Commentary*. Grand Rapids, MI: Eerdmans, 1992.

Mounce, William D., ed. *Mounce's Complete Expository Dictionary of Old and New Testament Words*. Grand Rapids, MI: Zondervan, 2006.

Newman, Barclay M., and Philip C. Stine. *A Handbook on the Gospel of Matthew*. New York: United Bible Societies, 1988.

Osborne, Grant R. "Matthew." *Zondervan Exegetical Commentary on the New Testament*. Grand Rapids, MI: Zondervan, 2010.

Phillips, John. *Acts 1-12*. Vol. 1 of *Exploring Acts*. Chicago, IL: Moody, 1986.

Sanders, E. P. *Jesus and Judaism*. London: SC Press, 1985.

Sarna, Nahum M. *Exodus*. The JPS Torah Commentary Series. Philadelphia, PA: Jewish Publication Society, 1991.

Saracco, Norberto. "The Holy Spirit and the Church's Mission of Healing." *International Review of Mission* 93 (July-October 2004): 413-420.

Schleirmacher, Friedrich. *The Life of Jesus*. Philadelphia, PA: Fortress, 1975.

Spencer, F. Scott. "Exorcism." In *The New Interpreters Dictionary of the Bible*, edited by Katharine Doob Sakenfeld, 383-385. Nashville, TN: Abingdon, 2007.

Stedman Ray C. *Hebrews*. The IVP New Testament Commentary Series. Downers Grove, IL: InterVarsity Press, 1992.

Story, J. Lyle. "Mark." In *The New Spirit-Filled Life Bible*, ed. Jack W. Hayford, 1380. Nashville, TN: Thomas Nelson Publishers, 2002.

Stulac, George M. *James*. The IVP New Testament Commentary Series. Downers Grove, IL: InterVarsity Press, 1993.

Talbert Charles T. *Reading Luke: A Literary and Theological Commentary on the Third Gospel.* New York: Crossroad, 1992.

Trapnell, D. H. "Healing—Its Meaning." In *The New Bible Dictionary*, 3rd ed., edited by I. Howard Marshall, A. R. Millard, J. I. Packer, and D. J. Wiseman, 452-453. Downers Grove, IL: InterVarsity, 1996.

Turner, David L. *Matthew.* Baker Exegetical Commentary on the New Testament. Grand Rapids, MI: Baker, 2008.

Twelftree, Graham H. *Jesus the Miracle Worker: A Historical and Theological Study.* Downers Grove, IL: InterVarsity Press, 1999.

———. *In the Name of Jesus: Exorcism Among the Early Christians.* Grand Rapids, MI: Baker Academic, 2007.

———. "Miracles in Mark." In *The New Dictionary of Biblical Theology*, edited by T. Desmond Alexander, Brian Rosner, D. A. Carson, and Graeme Goldsworthy, 777. Downers Grove, IL: InterVarsity, 2000.

Weirsbe, Warren. "The Prayer of Faith." In *James.* Vol. 2 of *The Bible Exposition Commentary: An Exposition of the New Testament Comprising the Entire "Be" Series. Matthew through Revelation.* Colorado Springs, CO: Cook Communications, 1989.

Whitacre Rodney A. *John.* The IVP New Testament Commentary Series. Downers Grove, IL: InterVarsity Press, 1999.

Wimber John. *Power Evangelism.* Rev. ed. London: Hodder & Stoughton, 1992.

Witherington, Ben, III. *Matthew.* Smyth and Helwys Bible Commentary. Macon, GA: Smyth and Helwys, 2006.

Yeboah, Charles. "Exorcism." In *Eerdmans' Dictionary of the Bible*, edited by David Noel Freedman, 444. Grand Rapids, MI: Eerdmans, 2000.

FURTHER SOURCES CONSULTED FOR PART TWO

Ahn, Che. *How to Pray for Healing: Understanding and Releasing the Healing Power Available to Every Christian*. Ventura, CA: Regal Books, 2004.

Aker, Benny C. *The Other Side of Signs and Wonders: Act 3:1-10 A Ministry Model for All Times*. [Dr. Aker emailed this to me in July of 2010]

Betty, L. Stafford. "The Growing Evidence for 'Demonic Possession': What Should Psychiatry's Response Be?" *Journal of Religion and Health*. 44 no 1 (Spring 2005): 13-30.

Bosworth, F. F. *Christ the Healer*. Grand Rapids, MI: Chosen Books, 1924.

Brown, Candy Gunther. "From Tent Meetings and Store-front Healing Rooms to Walmarts and the Internet: Healing Spaces in the United States, the Americas, and the World, 1906-2006." *Church History*. 75 no 3 (S 2006): 631-647.

Burkholder, Lawrence. "The Theological Foundations of Deliverance Healing." In *Conrad Grebel Review* 19, no. 1 (Winter 2001): 38-68.

Colbert, Don. *Deadly Emotions: Understand the Mind-Body-Spirit Connection that Can Heal or Destroy You*. Nashville, TN: Thomas Nelson, 2003.

Cox, Harvey. *Fire from Heaven: The Rise of Pentecostal Spirituality and the Reshaping of Religion in the Twenty-First Century*. Cambridge, MA: Da Capo Press, 1995.

Deiros, Pablo, and Pablo Bottari. "Deliverance from Dark Strongholds." In *Power, Holiness and Evangelism: Rediscovering God's Purity, Power and*

Passion for the Lost, compiled by Randy Clark, 109-118. Shippensburg, PA: Destiny Image, 1999.

Dickerman, Don. *When Pigs Move In: How to Clean the Demonic Influences Impacting Your Life and the Lives of Others*. Lake Mary, Florida, ST: Charisma House, 2009.

Ervin, Howard M. *Healing: Sign of the Kingdom*. Peabody, MA: Hendrickson Publishers, 2002.

Gaiser, Frederick J. "Healing in the Bible: A Grateful Response." *Journal of Pentecostal Theology,* 21, Issue 1 (April 1, 2012): 41-63.

Garlow, James. *God Still Heals*. Indianapolis, IN: Wesleyan Publishing House, 2005.

Grundmann, Christoffer H. "He Sent Them out to Heal! Reflections on the Healing Ministry of the Church." *Currents in Theology and Mission.* 33 no 5 (October 2006): 372-378.

Hamm, Dennis. "The Ministry of Deliverance and the Biblical Data." In *Deliverance Prayer*, edited by Matthew Linn and Dennis Linn. Ramsey, NJ: Paulist Press, 1980.

Hammond, Frank, and Ida Mae Hammond. *Pigs in the Parlor: A Practical Guide to Deliverance.*
Kirkwood, MO: Impact Books, 1973.

Hiers, Richard H. "Binding and Loosing: The Matthean Authorizations." In *Journal of Biblical Literature* 104, no. 2 (June 1985): 233-250.

Horrobin, Peter. *Healing Through Deliverance*. Vol. 1. of *The Foundation of Deliverance Ministry*. Grand Rapids, MI: Chosen Books, 1991.

———. *Healing Through Deliverance*. Vol. 2. of *The Foundation of Deliverance Ministry*. Grand Rapids, MI: Chosen Books, 2003.

Johnson, Bill, and Randy Clark. *The Essential Guide to Healing: Equipping All Christians to Pray for the Sick*. Bloomington, MN: Chosen Books, 2011.

Keener, C. S. "Cultural Comparisons for Healing and Exorcism Narratives in Matthew's Gospel."
In *HTS Teologiese Studies/Theological Studies* 66, no. 1 (July 28, 2010): 1-7.

Keener, Craig S. *Miracles: The Credibility of the New Testament Accounts*. Grand Rapids, MI: Baker Academic. 2011.

Koeng, Harold G., and Harvey Jay Cohen, eds. *The Link between Religion and Health: Psychoneuroimmunology and the Faith Factor*. Oxford, UK: University Press, 2002.

Kraft, Charles H. *Christianity with Power: Your Worldview and Your Experience of the Supernatural*. Eugene, OR: Wipf and Stock Publishers, 1989.

Kuhlman, Kathryn. *I Believe in Miracles*. Rev. ed. S. Plainfield, NJ: Bridge Publishing, 1992.

Laar, Wout van. "Churches as Healing Communities: Impulses from the South for an Integral Understanding of Healing." *Exchange*. 35 no 2 (2006): 226-241.

Lim, David. *Spiritual Gifts: A Fresh Look*. Springfield, MO: Gospel Publishing House, 1991.

Lozano, Neal. *Unbound: A Practical Guide to Deliverance*. Grand Rapids, MI: Chosen Books, 2003.

Ma, Wonsuk. "A 'First Waver' Looks at the 'Third Wave:' A Pentecostal Reflection on Charles Kraft's Power Encounter Terminology." In *Pneuma: The Journal of the Society for Pentecostal Studies* 19, no. 2 (1997): 189-206.

MacNutt, Francis. *Deliverance from Evil Spirits*. Grand Rapids, MI: Baker Publishing, 2009.

———. *Healing*. Notre Dame, IN: Ave Maria Press, 1999.

———. *Reawakening*. Grand Rapids, MI: Chosen Books, 2005.

———. *The Prayer that Heals: Praying for Healing in the Family*. Rev. ed. Notre Dame, IN:
Ave Maria Press, 2005.

Martin, Dale Basil. "When Did Angels Become Demons?" *Journal of Biblical Literature*. 129, Issue 4 (Winter 2010): 657-677.

McColl, Mary Ann, and Richard S. Ascough. "Jesus and People with Disabilities: Old Stories, New Approaches." *Journal of Pastoral Care & Counseling* 63 no 3-4 (Fall/Winter 2009): 1-11.

Miskov, Jennifer A. "Carrie Judd Montgomery: A Passion for Healing and the Fullness of the Spirit." *AG Heritage* 32 (2012): 4-12.

Montgomery, Carrie Judd. *The Prayer of Faith*. Memphis, TN: Bottom of the Hill Publishing, 2011.

Mraida, Carlos. "Inner Healing to Live in Freedom." In *Power, Holiness and Evangelism: Rediscovering God's Purity, Power and Passion for the Lost*, compiled by Randy Clark, 99-108. Shippensburg, PA: Destiny Image, 1999.

Murray, Andrew. *Divine Healing*. Springdale, PA: Whitaker House, 1982.

Pierce, Cal. *Healing in the Kingdom: How the Power of God and Your Faith Can Heal the Sick.*
Ventura, CA: Regal Books, 2008.

Poloma, Margaret M. *Main Street Mystics: The Toronto Blessing and Reviving Pentecostalism.*
Oxford, UK: AltaMira Press, 2003.

———. "Old Wine, New Wineskins: The Rise of Healing Rooms in Revival Pentecostalism." *Pneuma: The Journal of the Society of Pentecostal Studies* 28: no. 1 (Spring 2006): 59-71.

Prince, Derek. *They Shall Expel Demons: What You Need to Know about Demons—Your Invisible Enemies*. Grand Rapids, MI: Chosen Books, 1998.

Sanford, Agnes. *The Healing Light*. New York: Random House, 1947.

Saracco, Norberto. "The Holy Spirit and the Church's Mission of Healing." *International Review of Mission* 93, no. 370-371 (July-October 2004): 413-420.

Shelton, James B. "A Reply to Keith Warrington's Response to 'Jesus and Healing: Yesterday and Today.'" *Journal of Pentecostal Theology* 16, Issue 2 (April 2008): 113-117.

Simpson, A. B. *The Gospel of Healing*. Rev. ed. Camp Hill, PA: Wingspread Publishers, 2006.

Talbert, Charles T. *Reading Luke: A Literary and Theological Commentary on the Third Gospel.*
New York: Crossroad, 1992.

Theron, Jacques. "A Critical Overview of the Church's Ministry of Deliverance from Evil Spirits." *Pnuema: The Journal of the Society for Pentecostal Studies* 18, no. 1 (Spring 1996): 79-92.

Thomas, John Christopher. "Frederick J. Gaiser, *Healing in the Bible: Theological Insight for Christian Ministry* (Grand Rapids: Baker Academic, 2010) - An Appreciative Engagement." *Journal of Pentecostal Theology* 21 Issue 1 (April 2012): 16-26.

———. "Healing in the Atonement: A Johannine Perspective." *Journal of Pentecostal Theology* 14, Issue 1 (October 2005): 23-39.

Twelftree, Graham. *In the Name of Jesus: Exorcism among the Early Christians.* Grand Rapids, MI: Baker Academic, 2007.

Valloton, Kris. *Spirit Wars: Winning the Invisible Battle against Sin and the Enemy.* Minneapolis, MN: Baker Books, 2012.

Vann Laar, Wout. "Churches as Healing Communities: Impulses from the South for an Integral Understanding of Healing." *Exchange* 35, no. 2 (2006): 226-241.

Venter, Alexander. *Doing Healing: How to Minister God's Kingdom in the Power of the Spirit.*
Cape Town, South Africa: Vineyard International Publishing, 2009.

Wagner, C. Peter. *How to Have a Healing Ministry in Any Church: A Comprehensive Guide.*
Ventura, CA: Regal Books, 1988.

———. *Spiritual Warfare Strategy: Confronting Spiritual Powers.* Shippensburg, PA: Destiny Image, 1996.

Wagner, C. Peter, and John Dawson. *Territorial Spirits: Practical Strategies for How to Crush the Enemy through Spiritual Warfare.* Shippensburg, PA: Destiny Image, 2012. Kindle e-book.

Walaskay, Paul W. "Biblical and Classical Foundations of the Healing Ministries." *Journal of Pastoral Care* 37, no. 3 (1983) 195-206.

Warrington, Keith. "Reflections on the History and Development of Demonological Beliefs and Praxis Among British Pentecostals." *Asian Journal of Pentecostal Studies* 7, no. 2 (2004): 281-304.

Wigglesworth, Smith. *Wigglesworth on the Anointing.* New Kensington, PA: Whitaker House, 2000.

Wimber, John. *Power Evangelism.* Rev. ed. London: Hodder & Stoughton, 1992.

Wimber, John, and Kevin Springer. *Power Healing.* New York: HarperCollins, 1987.

Woodworth-Etter, Maria. *Signs and Wonders.* New Kensington, PA: Whitaker House, 1997.

Made in the USA
San Bernardino, CA
29 June 2016